Christopher was educated at Bradfield College in Berkshire and at The Royal Military Academy, Sandhurst.

After a brief but very worthwhile spell in the Army, he chose a change in career to become a chartered surveyor – thereafter spending the next 47 years writing condition reports on such properties as Georgian rectories, 17th century farmhouses and period cottages, for dewy-eyed clients intending to buy them!

Now, in his early seventies, Christopher has finally realised that writing children's stories is far more fun and much more interesting – beautifully illustrated by his wife, Sandy.

However, this was interrupted in December 2020 when their much-loved whippet-cross Scallywag died suddenly.

Christopher and Sandy were grief-stricken, and Christopher found that the only way of dealing with his grief was to write about her, revisiting happy memories.

This book is the result, a tribute to honour a beloved friend who came into Christopher's life at a critical time for him, likewise for Scallywag who was in need of a loving home. It is also to safeguard many precious memories of happy times together at home and aboard their narrowboat "Bluebell" on the Kennet & Avon Canal – and later on March Hare.

From the age of 16, Christopher spent much leisure time during his life on boats, crewing on a variety of yachts belonging to friends of his – sailing to the Channel Islands, to the north coast of Brittany, to the Scilly Isles and along the south-west coast of England, also taking part in the "Round the Island Race", circumnavigating the Isle of Wight.

These days, it is the gentler pace of the Kennet & Avon Canal and the beauty of its surrounding countryside that tempt Christopher to leave his laptop in favour of spending time on his cabin cruiser in the Somerset Coal Canal, one of the loveliest linear marinas in the south of England, just off the K&A.

This book is dedicated to the many organisations that rescue and re-home animals in need of love and care, and a fresh start.

Scallywag was one of those animals and I'm so very glad we met!

For those who are used to keeping a dog in the family, over the years there is usually one that stands out – a very special companion – and having had a series of whippet-crosses, Scallywag has been my special "stand-out" dog.

So, thank you for giving us the chance to enjoy what has been a wonderful life together!

Christopher Weedon

SCALLYWAG – MY DUVET DIVA

A doggy life lived to the full, ashore and afloat

AUSTIN MACAULEY PUBLISHERS™

LONDON • CAMBRIDGE • NEW YORK • SHARJAH

A CIP catalogue record for this title is available from the British Library.

ISBN 9781398453630 (Paperback)
ISBN 9781398453647 (ePub e-book)

www.austinmacauley.com

First Published 2022
Austin Macauley Publishers Ltd®
1 Canada Square
Canary Wharf
London
E14 5AA

With thanks to my dear wife Sandy, for taking Scallywag to her heart when she and I first met and for loving her too.

Also, for keeping me supplied with mugs of coffee – and boxes of tissues to enable me to see the keys as I typed!

Table of Contents

Prologue
The Last Goodbye

"Oh, thank goodness!"

The surgery door has opened and the lady vet looking after me has walked in, followed by Daddy – my master – come to take me home.

I'm warm, lying on a sheepskin on a bean bag, with a light blanket laid over me. The only trouble is, it's so hard to breathe and it hurts, Daddy, it hurts so much.

I try to wag my tail and to get up. But I'm so so sleepy. All I can do is to look up at Daddy with all the joy and love in my eyes that I can muster – so that he knows I'm so pleased to see him.

He walks over to me lying in my big cage with the door open. He kneels and takes my head in his hands, stroking the top of my head, my face, my ears and looks into my eyes. He tells me gently to 'stay'. "It's time for bye-byes, just go to sleep now and you'll soon feel better".

The kindly nurse steps forward and attaches something to my front leg, where there is a bandage, then steps back again behind my daddy.

He is still on his knees murmuring all the things he says to me at bedtime each night. I play our blinking game to tell him how much I love him and Daddy blinks back, as he always does. I feel very calm, very peaceful, but I must keep looking at Daddy so he knows I love him, must keep looki...

Part One

Eight Years Earlier
Monday, 16th January 2012

Following a three-hour drive and several wrong turns whilst trying to interpret Miss Athill's directions, I finally arrived at what must be my destination.

It was not encouraging – a tiny little end of terraced two up-two down red brick Victorian cottage on the edge of Birmingham, bordering what was obviously a trading estate. The threadbare curtains looked dirty, the window panes were grimy and one was broken – boarded up with some cardboard.

I had been thinking of getting a dog for some time. I was living alone following what I thought was a reasonably happy marriage – until in 2009 my then wife decided she wanted a change of scene, a change of lifestyle and whilst she was at it, a change of man for good measure. Upset as I was at the time, I am genuinely pleased to hear from acquaintances that she's happy.

But now, after three years of my own company, I was lonely.

Following the financial crash of 2008 four years earlier, I had lost my house trying to save the business in which I was an unlimited liability partner with five others.

I was therefore living temporarily in my late mother's top floor flat in Wincanton which she had left to my sister in Australia and which we were trying to sell.

Thinking of the future, a permanent home for myself and the little that I could afford, I had experienced a light-bulb moment – which led me to buying a narrow boat on the Kennet & Avon Canal to live on during my retirement – which was looming.

Actually, I was rather looking forward to a complete change of scene too. It would be an adventure. However, I hankered for company.

I had lost not only my house but my last whippet-cross to kidney failure four years ago. 2008/9 had been dreadful years for me – and for many others. Now enough time had elapsed for me to consider another dog.

The human company had not worked. Dogs were unconditionally loyal and trustworthy – in my experience.

So, I started looking. I visited several rescue centres searching for another whippet-cross – a small narrow dog for a small narrow boat. My last companion – the dog, that is – had been gentle, affectionate and easy to live with and I had resolved to have a whippet-cross again. I even agreed to adopt a small lurcher – but on the drive home I decided she was just too big for the confines of my boat.

A friend mentioned a helpful website for those looking to adopt a dog.

I logged on and down the left-hand side of the screen were listed all the breeds looking for a home. I clicked onto "Whippet-cross" and that was how I found "Sally".

She was a honey-coloured "10-month-old whippet-cross bitch, affectionate with a quiet nature, good with children and other dogs". She looked adorable in the photograph and just the right size for my new floating accommodation. However, after a much earlier marital break-up in my more distant past, I would have to change Sally's name. Still fond of my former wife, it would have felt odd to be constantly calling her name when summoning my dog!

I called the telephone number and found myself talking to Miss Athill, Sally's foster carer. Having answered a lot of her probing questions, I was told I sounded suitable, but given that I was living in Wincanton – nearly three hours' drive away – the rescue centre would not be able to send anybody to inspect where Sally was going to live.

She suggested that, instead, I should obtain a reference from the vets who had been looking after my last dog and should bring it with me when I came to inspect Sally.

The reference was duly obtained – and now here I was, sitting outside Miss Athill's run-down cottage, clutching the necessary passport to what I hoped would be my future companion – and happiness.

Miss Athill answered my knock, as did what sounded like a pack of dogs somewhere in the back of the little house, all barking their heads off. She showed me into her downstairs bed-sitting room, sparsely furnished without a sofa, just one easy chair, a small table with two upright chairs and an old single wrought iron bed, covered with a bright orange candlewick bedspread. A meagre fire flickered in the grate.

Clearly, Miss Athill had a kind and loving heart. I suspected she was spending most of what she had on her canine charges.

Having scanned my reference, Miss Athill asked me to wait. She would bring Sally in to see me.

After a moment or two, the door opened and Sally enthusiastically entered the room, pulling Miss Athill behind her on a lead. I knelt down on one knee to Sally's level, to say hello.

In terms of size, she was all that I was hoping for. But I did not have long to worry about that – or anything else. The next moment both her front legs were around my neck, my face was being licked all over, her tail was wagging furiously, and I felt my left foot suddenly become warm and rather wet. She had peed on me with excitement!

"OH YESSS! I DO like him. Maybe he's going to adopt me! Please take me away from here."

Any lingering doubts were dispelled immediately. I had found my future companion!

After a brief chat with Miss Athill, I made what I hoped would be regarded as a generous donation and we said goodbye. I loaded Sally into the car for our three-hour return trip to Wincanton, turning south to join the M5. I had left Wincanton soon after lunch, but it was now nearly 6 p.m.

It was a filthy evening, dark by now and sheeting with rain.

I began to think over what Miss Athill had told me of Sally's past.

She couldn't tell me much. Apparently, Sally had been found thin, bedraggled, hungry and frightened wandering alone close to the centre of Birmingham. Miss Athill thought she must have been dumped – and had been looking after her for nearly two months. Despite what had happened to her, I was told Sally had an affectionate nature and had responded well to kindness, company and good food.

"Oh no! I don't feel well at all. I feel SO sick. I want us to stop."

What sort of people could *do* that to a dog who was little more than a puppy?

Later in our time together, I was to discover she remained anxious if we were out and about together on a walk and she lost me. Her early experience had clearly been a very frightening time for her.

My musings were abruptly interrupted by the sound of Sally swallowing hard and clearly about to be sick. Sure enough, she produced a torrent of vomit – and I cursed Miss Athill for having fed her shortly before I arrived for our meeting. Sally was going to be facing a long drive home and a meal just beforehand was inviting car sickness.

My poor girl continued to be sick into her bed and obviously hated lying in it – a veritable sea of vomit by the time we got home. However, there was little I could do about it. It was kinder to press on and to get the journey over with as soon as possible. All I could do was to talk to her.

"UGH! YUCK! This is HORRIBLE! Don't just talk to me. Stop and clean me up. PLEASE, why can't we STOP?"

I also wondered what have I done – adopting a dog that is perhaps car sick? My job surveying houses took me out and about, involving a fair bit of driving and it would be difficult to cope with her if she was going to be one of those dogs that are forever car sick. I resolved to drive slowly like a nervous granny for the next couple of weeks in the hope of giving Sally her confidence back and of preventing a repeat of what we were going through right now.

Finally, we were home. It was just after 9 p.m. I resolved to put Sally's sheepskin bed straight into the washing machine and Sally herself into a lukewarm bath. But first, she needed a little run on some grass to spend a penny.

"Oh, thank goodness I'm out of that awful smelly filth and the journey's over! I'm bursting now, I need to do a wee – and quickly!"

That done, she followed me meekly into the building and across the hall to the lifts. She had clearly never been in a lift before and was *very* suspicious of this huge box I was trying to coax her into. I went in first and knelt down on one knee as I had done before and after a moment or two, she crawled into it on her tummy.

"This seems such a kind man, but WHY does he want me to go into this enormous silver box? It looks like Miss Athill's oven, only a lot cleaner and a lot bigger. I don't want to be cooked, thank you! Oh well, do I have any choice?" "I suppose I will have to trust him."

She lay on the floor of the lift, shaking slightly, whilst I made a fuss of her. The lift negotiated, we went down the passage to the front door of my flat and went in. Sally was quite happy wandering around the flat sniffing everything, whilst I ran a lukewarm bath for her.

Bless her, she let me lift her into the water without struggling and then stood stock still whilst I soaped her and then rinsed her down with the hand-shower. I was talking to her all the time. I think my voice calmed her – and that she was enjoying it!

"Oooh, this is lovely! I've never had this before! I feel so warm and clean again and I don't smell anymore. This man seems to really like me, to take care of me like this. I hope he's going to let me stay here with him?"

Once I had towelled her dry, I gave her a little rice and cooked chicken to settle her tummy, which she wolfed down looking around for more.

"Mmm, THAT was yummy. I'm SO hungry now – is there anymore, anymore at all, please?"

With Sally's basket in the washing machine, I laid a blanket on the carpet for her beside the sofa where I sat to have my supper. Sally didn't think much of this idea and promptly hopped up beside me and lay down.

"You MUST be joking! I'm a whippet-cross and I like my home comforts!"

There was much the same problem when I went to bed. Without a basket, Sally obviously wondered where was she supposed to sleep for the night. After taking her outside for her last penny (carrying her into the lift), I encouraged her back onto her blanket and gave her a little treat, telling her she *must* be tired and it was time to go to sleep.

"Do you REALLY think I'm going to stay here on this blanket all night? I DON'T think so!"

Silly me!

Starting Our Life Together – Tuesday 17th January 2012

Next morning, I awoke to find Sally stretched out beside me, part under the duvet, with her head on the pillow, watching me!

"Oooh, this is SO warm and comfortable. I love it here. Please don't push me out and make me go next door!"

Oh well, the training might have gone out of the window almost immediately upon our acquaintance – but at least she was evidently feeling secure with me!

One of the great things about being a surveyor is that you spend so much time out of the office. In consequence, save for my loyal secretaries very few people ever knew exactly where I was during working hours.

Yesterday I had been in the office for most of the morning catching up on reports, before collecting the reference from the vet and thereafter driving north to meet Sally in Birmingham.

However, I had earlier had the foresight to book myself an official day off for today – Tuesday. I wanted a little time to get to know Sally and to give her the chance to relax a bit in her new environment.

Clearly, she was relaxed already!

Time to get up and to take Sally outside. I pulled on my dressing gown, noting that the newspaper I had put down for her the night before remained dry.

Miss Athill had warned me that Sally was not entirely house trained, so grabbing a roll of paper towels, in case of an accident in the lift or in the main hall, we wasted no time in finding a convenient patch of grass outside. Sally didn't seem to worry about the lift this morning. Maybe it was because she was bursting. The moment she found the right spot she squatted for what seemed enough time to fill a reservoir!

"Oooooh! That's good! I really needed that! I didn't think I was going to make it." That feels SO much better!

I made a huge fuss of her and I must have looked a bit odd to anyone glancing out of the window or passing by – a man in a dressing gown so excited and in raptures because his dog had spent a penny!

On our return, Sally wasn't so sure about the lift. However, our lovely House Manager, Sue, was about to use it and practically fell on Sally with enthusiasm, stroking her ears and patting her, holding her head in her hands and looking into her eyes, telling her how beautiful she was and asking if she could take Sally home with her!

"Oooh, I could get used to this! This seems a nice lady! She likes me too! But I really think I'd rather stay with this man who came and fetched me and brought me here – even if he did make me dreadfully sick on the way and wouldn't stop. He gave me such a nice warm bath afterwards and has looked after me so well, I've forgiven him. So, I hope he doesn't give me to her!"

Once back in the flat I gave Sally her breakfast and went off to shave and shower.

Upon returning to my bedroom, I found Sally reclining on the duvet, looking like the Queen of Sheba. This time I gently told her that she must wait for me on her blanket and gently led her into the sitting room, saw her settled and shut the door.

"Oh well, it was worth a try!"

When I returned for my breakfast, Sally was curled up in a ball on the sofa, her nose under her tail and one beady eye fixed on me. She wasn't stupid! She was clearly waiting to see my reaction.

"So, what are you going to do now?"

I gently returned her to her blanket, thinking I must collect her sheepskin bed from the laundry room, following its double-wash and dry – after poor Sally's sickness, during our long journey home yesterday evening.

After breakfast, I tried a little test. I left the sitting room door into our hall open, telling Sally I would be back in a minute – before I departed through the front door, leaving her alone in the flat. I wanted her to see me leave and to find out if she would bark in my absence.

I made it to the lift without a sound from her and when I returned with her bed nearly 10 minutes later, again there was no sound and she was lying in the hall of the flat, waiting for me.

I got a disproportionately over-excited welcome from her, tail wagging furiously and she even *talked* to me in doggy talk – better than widdling all over my foot!

"Oh, I'm SO glad you're back. I didn't know if you were going to come back. I thought perhaps you had left me here, maybe forever. I'm SO relieved to see you – and I was good, wasn't I – not barking?"

I was thrilled too. Not only did she appear to have accepted me as her new Master, but she hadn't barked. This was important as inevitably I would have to leave her on her own sometimes, in the office or in the car. She got almost as rapturous a reaction *from* me, as she had given *to* me.

"Oh, he DOES seem pleased with me!"

Next on the agenda was a walk.

It was a bright winter's morning after the rain of last night and we set off across the town centre car park in front of the flats and up a grassed area to one side, set about with bench-tables. It was a little bit of parkland for people to relax in on spring or summer days and to enjoy a family picnic or to meet up with friends.

Sally hadn't hesitated to enter the lift this time and though excited to be going out for a walk, she didn't pull too much on the lead. At the top of the grassed area with benches was a stone and timber stile. I climbed over and Sally squeezed underneath.

We were in a field that followed the lie of the land, still sloping uphill to a ridge. Cresting the ridge, we could look down on further pasture, some woodland bordering the road to Bruton and enjoy a fine view of Wincanton Racecourse beyond. During the national hunt season, this was a good place to sit and to get a free view of the racing through a pair of binoculars.

However, Sally wasn't interested in the view. Just below us was a herd of cows, black and white Friesians, some grazing, others lying down, all enjoying the winter sunshine. Sally stopped dead, let out a nervous "woof", then turned tail and tried to flee back to the flat.

"OH NO! WHAT are those? They're huge. I've never seen anything like them before. They look so fierce – I'm off. I'm not hanging around here!"

I had her on the lead – so she didn't get far. I was warned to keep her on a lead for the first two to three weeks until she knew me and until I was confident that she would come back to me when called. Basic stuff as I had kept a dog before – but good advice.

Sally was clearly both surprised and frightened by the cows. I wondered if perhaps in her young life she had ever met a cow before. If not, I was not surprised at her reaction. I knelt beside her with my arm around her and tried to quietly re-assure her. She calmed down a little but kept up a growling noise in her throat.

"It's all very well, cuddling me and talking to me. But how do you know those big creatures aren't going to get up and chase us? I really DON'T like this AT ALL. I'm frightened."

She was not at all sure what these huge black and white creatures were – and the trouble with cows is that they are naturally inquisitive! One or two started to move towards us and Sally tried to make another run for it. This time she nearly slipped her collar and I was lucky not to lose her.

"OH NO! They are getting ready to chase us! I'm getting out of here!"

We beat a tactical retreat, skirting around the herd – Sally never taking her eyes of the cows for a moment.

"I don't trust them!"

Walking on down the hill we negotiated another stile, this time without cows awaiting us in the next field. This bordered the woodland that we had seen from above and we encountered some rabbits – and a couple of squirrels teasingly dancing over the ground right in front of us before racing up into the trees.

The cows now forgotten, Sally was fascinated by the wildlife. She stood stock-still watching the rabbits – but the movement of the squirrels had her lurching forward, ready to give chase until brought up short by her lead.

"OH WOW! That's a bit more like it! I want to catch one of them! PLEASE let me off this wretched lead. How do you expect me to be able to chase them, tied to you?"

Well, she might be a bit timid now, but she was not short of natural instinct. I would have to watch her with cats.

Below us lay a stream and the path beside it, leading back into the town. We followed this, meeting another dog on a lead alongside a pushchair, with a young mother in charge. We stepped aside to let the little cavalcade pass. The little boy in the pushchair put his hand out to Sally who pulled forward to see what she was being offered.

"Mmm, what's he got for me? He smells of jam! He tastes of jam! Yum yum!"

All she wanted to do was to lick him, first his hand then his face. I remembered Miss Athill saying Sally was good with children and I wondered whether she had belonged to a family before finding herself a stray.

Indeed, throughout her life, she rarely missed the opportunity to trot up to a child and give him or her "a kiss". Not always popular, particularly with grandparents, so I did my best to discourage it, putting her on her lead to avoid the inevitable "kissing-fest".

My theory was that small children sometimes have food all over their faces and Sally simply wanted what they had eaten for tea! But occasionally she knocked younger children over backwards and that really wasn't acceptable.

On our walk up the High Street, back to the flat, we called in at the pet shop. I wanted to buy Sally a warm waterproof coat, some sort of sheepskin or another soft basket for her comfort in the car, also some "toys" to play with. In addition, she needed an identification tag to go on her collar in case she got lost and I ordered her a doggy life jacket, also buying a beanbag for her to use on the boat.

She was much admired and indeed she was a *very* pretty dog.

The overall colour of warm honey, she nonetheless had a dark muzzle with the odd "beauty spot" on her cheek and on the front of her throat – each with a couple of black whiskers sticking out, something I found endearing.

Her ears were too big for a whippets' and when she was surprised or interested, they stood out like the handlebars of a bicycle on each side of her head. That said, they were incredibly soft to stroke and I soon came to admire the intricate folds inside her ears – rather like the mechanics of a foldaway car hood – with a line of very fine white fur along the front of the inside of each ear.

The fur on top of her head was wonderfully soft as well. The honey faded to a much lighter shade on her chest and she had white tips to her toes on each paw.

She had large liquid brown eyes and a permanent slightly anxious expression that would melt most hearts – certainly mine. There was a dark line extending back from each eye and later when I had re-married, I used to joke that Sally used to sit up under the duvet each morning with Sandy and they would put on their eye liner together.

And I loved her bottom! Again, her fur was much lighter and in whorls on each side, dark in their centres – so that with her darker striped tail between the two, they looked like two eyes staring at you divided by an elephant's trunk!

The lady running the pet shop fussed over Sally trying coats on her for size and helping me choose some soft bedding and several toys for her, plus filling out an order form for the tag and the lifejacket.

"Oooh, this is fun! Nobody's ever bought so many lovely things for me! I really think he likes me and wants to keep me. Maybe all my troubles are over at last? Maybe this is going to be my second chance? I can feel my heart bursting with love and gratitude for this kind man."

Later that afternoon was going to be a test – we had an eight-mile drive to Gillingham and after last night's car journey I was worried whether Sally would be car sick again.

I had booked an appointment with my former vet, Richard Gale, to get Sally registered, have her checked over, to obtain advice on inoculations and when I might have her spayed. My lifestyle would not have accommodated puppies and indeed when she was later spayed, Richard found that her uterus was exceptionally thin and she might well have died giving birth, had she had puppies.

Sally was naturally suspicious of the car after last night's dreadful journey and I had to lift her in.

"Oh NO! Not again! I really don't want to go in that awful machine that made me so sick. I DO SO HOPE he's not going

to take me back to Miss Athill's after all? I couldn't bear it. What have I done wrong?"

She was not keen to lie down in her new comfy bed and instead stood looking about her and trembling slightly. I sat in the drivers' seat with the engine running, talking quietly to her and stroking her and after a few minutes, she seemed a little calmer. I gave her a small biscuit bone to distract her and we set off.

I must have annoyed quite a lot of drivers that afternoon, as we travelled along at no more than 25–30 miles per hour, collecting a queue of cars, vans and lorries behind us. However, I was desperate to do all I could to avoid making Sally car sick.

She, meanwhile, had subsided into her bed. She wasn't asleep but lying with her head between her paws watching me as I occasionally glanced in the rear-view mirror (adjusted for the purpose).

We eventually arrived at the veterinary surgery and I breathed an enormous sigh of relief. Sally had not been sick and appeared to be perfectly calm. We were not out of the woods yet, but it was looking promising.

It suddenly occurred to me that Sally might have been bundled out of a car when dumped and perhaps that accounted for her reluctance to jump in earlier. There was so much I did not know about her and I would simply have to try to anticipate problems for her before they arose.

I encouraged Sally to spend a penny on the grass in front of the surgery before leading her into reception. She followed me in without hesitating and I was delighted how much she seemed to trust me already.

The receptionist and a nurse both knelt down to make an enormous fuss of her which was great. She was obviously enjoying all the attention, almost wagging her tail off her bottom and I wanted her to associate a visit to the vets with a good time. I did not want it to be a frightening place for her.

"Oh, THIS is fun! What lovely people! Maybe my nice Master isn't going to take me back to Miss Athill's after all. I DO so wish I knew what is going on and what's going to happen to me!"

I was given a clipboard with a registration questionnaire to fill in whilst we waited our turn to see Richard. The first question was "Name"?

I had been giving this some thought. I did not associate "Sally" with an altogether happy time in my life, but Sally had been a person whom I had loved. Time had healed us both, but nonetheless, I was uncomfortable with the name of Sally for my dog – for a person who had been special to me, yes that was fine – but not for a dog, however important it was to become in my life. "Sally" did not feel right and so I needed to change the name.

I was tempted to call my new companion "Nellie", as in "Nellie the Elephant", in honour of her bottom! However, I could not be that unkind. How could she go through life bearing a joke of a name at her own expense? She might not know that, but I would! Anyway, she was not really a "Nellie".

She obviously knew her name, so it seemed a pity to change it to something completely different.

In the end, I had decided on "Scally" – for two reasons. It sounded so similar to the name she knew that she wouldn't notice the difference. Also, she had to get used to so many sudden and major changes in her life, I reasoned that totally changing her name as well would only add to the bewilderment.

She'd already had to start getting used to living with me, in a flat and arriving and leaving in a lift. She would be coming to work with me in the office and out in the car when I would be surveying houses. And on top of that, she would be spending weekends with me on my narrow boat cruising the Kennet & Avon Canal – starting in four days' time!

I simply didn't want to cause her any more confusion than was absolutely necessary.

Within the next six months, she would be christened "Scallywag" due to her mischievous nature. It became her "official" name, but on an everyday basis she would be known as "Scally".

Finally, the surgery door opened and a young couple with an elderly Staffordshire bull terrier came out. The "Staffy" had a bandaged paw and a plastic "lampshade" around its neck. Whilst the couple waited to settle their bill at the reception desk, Richard beckoned me in.

One of the things I admired about Richard was his empathy with animals – something essential for a vet. He did not just dive in and get on with it. He always spent a few moments letting his patient get to know him to generate trust in the animal – particularly dogs.

I had seen it often before when bringing Sam, my last whippet-cross to him for treatment of his pads which kept growing corns, making walking painful.

Richard generated so much confidence in Sam that in the end, he would stand stock still on the table letting Richard cut out the corns with a sharp scalpel, without any form of anaesthetic.

Now, Richard sat on the floor and encouraged Scally to come to him. One thing I had already discovered about Scally was she liked a fuss being made of her. Although she had supposedly been dumped, she still liked – and seemed to trust – people.

She wasted no time in trying to give Richard a kiss, whilst her tail wagged furiously – so much so that her bottom wagged from side to side with it!

"Ooh, I like him! He wants to play with me. Well, I'm good at that. Let's go for it!!!"

In the end, once she had calmed down a bit, much of the examination was conducted at floor level.

Richard stroked her, feeling different parts of her body, he listened to her heartbeat and to her breathing and examined her ears, her teeth, her eyes and her pads.

Scally struggled a bit once or twice, but he quickly soothed her with his voice.

After taking her temperature, Richard pronounced himself well satisfied. True, he identified a slight heart murmur but he said she should grow out of that as her heart developed. I was not concerned as my last two whippet-crosses had each been diagnosed with the same thing at the late puppy stage and had gone on to lead perfectly healthy lives thereafter.

Her teeth, amongst other things, tended to confirm her age.

He thought she was a whippet probably crossed with a saluki, given her colouring, the shape of her ears and the way some of her fur grew on her body – and warned me she may be wilful and stubborn at times, a saluki trait apparently.

I had experienced this already, given Scally's determination to stealthily climb under my duvet on every possible occasion. Earlier at lunchtime, she had even stood at my closed bedroom door scratching it and whining, asking to be let in!

We discussed inoculations, when she could safely be spayed, worming, flea and tick control and other such matters, whilst Scally sniffed her way around Richard's surgery. He injected a tiny microchip into her neck to identify her in case she ever became lost, then gave her a small biscuit as a treat, saying he considered her a "cracker" (quite a good name, I thought!) and wishing me luck.

Having collected some medication to control worms and to discourage fleas etc. and chosen a travelling cage for the car, I paid our bill. Scally spent another penny on the grass outside and we headed for my office a mile away in the town.

I had realised long ago that the secret to housetraining a young dog is to anticipate when it might need to spend a penny – or more. By the time the dog lets you know, it is too late! As a result, we had very few "accidents" in the flat, on the boat, or elsewhere.

That said, when the staff came into my office to meet Scally, it was all too much for her and she did a small widdle of excitement on the carpet. Dee, my secretary, thought she was *adorable* and picked her up and cuddled her – just as well Scally's bladder was empty by that stage, otherwise Dee would have had the same treatment as my left foot had, yesterday!

"Oh Wow! All these lovely people making such a fuss of me. I'm beginning to feel quite special now, instead of being rejected and unwanted by everyone. This is SO wonderful!"

Dee's lovely yellow Labrador, Toby, came out from under her desk and, bless him, showed no sign of jealously, wagging his tail in welcome too and they were always firm friends whilst Dee was my secretary.

"And I like this other dog. He's so much bigger than me, but he seems so kind and gentle!"

I had wanted this little introduction today, as I was to be back at work tomorrow and it was a way of breaking Scally in gently. I also needed to collect a file with my notes proforma for tomorrow's survey.

Scally slept most of the way home, after all her excitement, but *much* more importantly showed no signs of feeling car sick.

Things were looking good! It must have been that meal that Miss Athill had given Scally shortly before my arrival that had caused her to be sick. Even so, I drove home in "granny" mode, again collecting a convoy of frustrated motorists behind me.

That evening turned out to be "lesson time" for both of us.

I had been talking to Scally a lot, to get her used to my voice and to establish her confidence. I wanted her to know that she was loved and safe with me, in her new home.

She had wolfed down her dinner of "complete" dry biscuit, with a little meat in jelly mixed in and I had taken her outside immediately afterwards to do her business.

Now I was in my little kitchenette off the sitting room cooking my own supper. I looked over to see what Scally was doing. She was lying on the carpet engrossed in chewing one of the legs of the dining table.

"*NO*", I said loudly. "*That's NAUGHTY! BAD Girl!*"

Scally had never heard me talk to like that before. She stopped what she was doing and looked up at me with big round eyes and her head down as if she knew she was in trouble. I stood over her and pointed at the table leg, again saying "*No. You must NOT chew Daddy's things!*"

"*Oh NO! I've upset my master. Oh dear! I hope he's not going to take me back to Miss Athill's now. I LIKE it here. I'm sorry. My teeth were hurting and I needed to chew on something – but I didn't think it would make you angry. Please, please forgive me, Master.*"

I doubt she understood exactly what I was on about, but she did realise she had done something wrong.

I didn't send her to her basket, as I did not want her to associate her basket with punishment. Instead, I sat down beside her on the floor and gave her one of her new toys , which were all lying beside her basket. It was a hard pink plastic bone with bobbles all over it. I told her to chew that instead.

I also told her that if she didn't chew my things, then I wouldn't chew hers!

"Oh, he's understood! He's given me this toy bone to chew instead, to stop my teeth from hurting. Perhaps he's not so angry as I thought – and maybe he'll let me stay here with him, after all. It's so lovely here. I don't want to go back to Miss Athill's."

I think that was almost the only time she attempted to chew something of mine. Knowledgeable and experienced dog trainers would probably criticise my words and my reaction, but I felt it was the firmest and the kindest response at the time – and it seemed to work.

I was on the receiving end of another lesson that evening.

I was tired after the long drive to Birmingham and back the day before and after the worry of trying to do all the right things for Scally.

I was sitting on the sofa watching telly, eating my supper and using the coffee table to rest my plate on... and fell asleep!

"Oooh, he's gone to sleep!... his supper smells lovely... maybe I'll take just a little mouthful to see what it tastes like and he won't notice. Mmmm, that's DELICIOUS! Just one more bite... ooh that's SO nice... I can't stop myself.

Oh dear, there's nothing left now – and I was licking the plate so hard, it's fallen on the carpet! Oh no, now I'm really for it!... maybe, when he wakes up, he won't remember and think he's already finished his supper! I'll pretend to be asleep!"

Upon waking – about 15 minutes later and in that split second before I opened my eyes – I thought *"Oh good. I'm still hungry and I've still got my supper to finish!"*

Not so! When I opened my eyes, my plate was upside down on the carpet and my knife and fork were scattered several feet away. There was no sign of any food, anywhere.

Scally must have eaten my remaining supper and in licking the plate clean had slid it sideways off the coffee table and onto the soft carpet. Even so, I must have been deeply asleep not to hear anything at all!

Now, Scally was fast asleep herself, doubtless dreaming of my shepherd's pie.

I could hardly blame Scally for what came naturally – after all she had been living in a pack of other dogs with Miss Athill, doubtless needing to grab whatever food came her way. She was a lurcher, a breed renown for stealing and I had put temptation right in front of her and at her height… stupid me!

Thereafter, throughout her life and latterly with Sandy, I had to ensure that all *our* food was either put away or well out of reach. Sometimes, our Sunday lunch would be barricaded behind a host of shiny saucepans before serving, likewise, the leftovers whilst they cooled.

Later that evening I faced another dilemma.

Where was Scally going to sleep? I was mindful of the rule *"start as you mean to go on",* which would have meant putting Scally in her basket in the sitting room and shutting the door.

The problem with that was twofold. At best she would stay in her basket, but a night curled up on the sofa was much more likely and/or a very scratched sitting-room door.

The alternative was to put her basket in my bedroom. She would feel more secure being close to me and I would have more control over her. The downside was that she would probably end up under the duvet with me, as she had done last night!

Did I mind? Not really. The chances of sharing my bed with human company within the foreseeable future seemed remote, Scally was a remarkably clean dog with short fine hair – and after her shower last night she smelled really quite acceptable! She would probably sleep on or under the duvet on the narrowboat anyway – as space was tight.

Oh well. I wasn't going to stress over everything. The last couple of days had been worrying enough – trying to find where to go in Birmingham, Scally's potential car sickness and simply trying to anticipate and to accommodate all her needs.

As I took her down in the lift for her last penny, before we went to bed, I concluded we would each find solutions that worked for us.

Part Two
And So, to Work

Next morning, I awoke to find Scally still in her basket beside my bed. I had conceived the bright idea of putting a woolly rug over her to keep her warm and so that maybe she would think she was under a duvet. It seemed to have worked. I was delighted!

Mind you, she was so pleased to see me awake she immediately hopped up on the bed and laid on top of the duvet on her back, wanting her tummy tickled. This was to prove a morning ritual throughout her life. I was relieved she was already so relaxed with me.

Morning, Daddy! I WAS good to stay in my bed, wasn't I? Please tickle my tummy – it feels SO nice and SO relaxing! Aaaah, that's perfect. You're SO good at it. Nobody has done this for me, for a VERY long time. I could lie here all day!

It was back to work today – another test for Scally.

After a quick trip outside for a penny etc., (no longer any hesitation with the lift) I gave Scally a small breakfast hopefully to avoid car sickness, dressed and ate mine, then set out for our morning walk. This was to become our routine, for years to come.

By 08:15, we were in the car, this time with Scally in her basket inside the large cage I had fitted yesterday – after buying it from the vets.

"Oh, I don't know about this! Why have I got to go in there? Will it stop me feeling sick? Will I fit inside it? I'm NOT happy, Master."

She was initially very reluctant to go into it, but I did not rush her, eventually coaxing her in with some tasty treats. After standing and whining for the first few minutes of our journey, she seemed to accept the cage and lay down with only a moan and a grunt of protest, then she was quiet.

"I suppose he's got his reasons for putting me in here, but I DON'T like it! I don't like it at all!"

We were heading south to an old rectory I was to survey – usually about a six-hour job. The owners were going to be there to let me in and to answer any questions before I started my inspection, and I wondered how Scally would take to being cooped up in the car for quite a while. I was also still worrying whether she would be car sick. She was lying on some newspaper in her basket just in case she was ill and I again drove slowly and sedately to reduce the risk.

I need not have worried. Scally had settled down for a snooze soon after we set off and did not move until I drove in through the rectory gates.

The owners came out to greet me as we pulled up and introductions over they "ooohed" and "aaahed" over my beautiful dog – pushing her nose against the bars of her cage, whining with excitement and tail wagging furiously.

"*Do* let her out," they said, "she can play with William," a rather handsome golden retriever standing by the car, also wagging his tail, having scented there was a dog in the car.

"Oh yes, DO, Daddy! I would love a game with William! Pleeeease!"

I had to explain that I had rescued Scally only two days ago and she needed to get used to staying in the car whilst I worked. I would not always be able to let her out to play and anyway I would be hard-pressed to concentrate on what I was doing if I was constantly worrying about where Scally was and what she was up to.

"I'll be good, I PROMISE!"

I felt a right spoilsport, but her training started *here*!

I told the owners I would be popping back to the car from time to time during the survey to check on Scally and, relenting a little, I suggested she might play with William when I had my lunch and I could keep an eye on her.

I unpacked my surveyors' ladder and other gear from the boot, also Scally's bobbly hard pink chew and a few other toys, hopefully to keep her amused in my absence and watched her as she settled down in her basket inside the cage, chewing the toy bone.

"Hmph! I suppose I'll have to put up with this! Please come back to me when you've finished. I don't like being left on my own!"

When I popped out of the house a little later to check on her, she was lying on her side, *fast* asleep.

Several more visits to the car confirmed the same thing – right up until nearly lunchtime. I suppose the events of the past couple of days had worn her out more than I had realised, both emotionally and physically.

And it also occurred to me – given that she might have been dumped from a car and left cold and hungry and alone – it was frankly miraculous that she wasn't barking for me, instead being calm and quiet. *What* a relief!

The survey was going well by the time I broke for lunch. The weather was overcast but dry and not too cold. I had completed my inspection of the outside of the house, the outbuildings and the drains and was part way through inspecting the interior – including the cellars and the roof spaces.

I enjoyed my job. Given that most houses are occupied and therefore carpeted and fully furnished when they are surveyed, you can only actually see about 65% of the structure. There may well be defects lurking out of sight, such as dry rot or dangerous electrical wiring, so you need to look for the secondary clues indicating such issues – rather like a game of detection. At that stage, with just over 40 years of practical surveying behind me, I was really quite good at detection!

Also, as I've mentioned already, you are out and about much more than spending time in the office, you can organise your day, and no two days are ever the same.

So, all was going well both in respect of the survey and more importantly, Scally!

She stood up in her cage as I approached the car, wagging her tail and looking expectant.

"Oh, hello, Daddy! You've come back! Are you going to let me out? Where are we going now?"

I got her out of the car for a run – still on her lead of course – and a little way down the lane she obligingly did all her business, ready for the afternoon's confinement.

I ate my lunch sitting on a hay bale in the stable yard. This was enclosed, so I was able to let Scally off the lead and she had a great game with William.

She was a little in awe of him to start with, but soon realised he was a gentle giant – so that they spent much of the time taking it in turns to chase each other around the yard. William found a stick and they then had a tug of war. William, being the heavier, easily pulled Scally this way and that accompanied by ferocious growling from both dogs – and wagging of tails, at the same time!

"OOOH, this is GREAT!!! I do like William! He's so big, but he's fun! Please can we take him home with us, so I've got someone to play with?"

After about half an hour of this, Scally was exhausted, lying there panting with her tongue lolling out. When she had got her breath back, I gave both dogs some water and put Scally back in her cage, in the car.

"It's OK, Daddy. You go off and do your thing. I'm shattered!"

I stayed with her for a few minutes to see her settled, by which time she was flat out, fast asleep, exhausted from her lunchtime games!

By 3 p.m., the light was beginning to fade.

I had finished my survey. The necessary photographs had been taken, and I loaded all my survey gear back into the boot of my car.

Scally was standing in her cage, wagging her tail and whining to be let out.

"YAY!!! You're back! Where's my new friend William?"

Hooking her onto the lead, I walked her down the drive and once more out into the lane for another penny, then loaded her up and having said good-bye to the rectory owners, I set off for my office in Gillingham.

"Daddy, STOP! We've left William behind!"

Again, I drove sympathetically, taking corners slowly, likewise pulling away and stopping gently. My lovely girl was wide awake but wasn't sick – *thank goodness!* I thought again, even if I have to drive around this slowly for the rest of her life, I'll gladly do it to avoid her being ill.

My secretaries shared the job of working for me and this afternoon it was Ann on duty (without a dog). She made a great fuss of Scally and as before most of the front office staff drifted in to say hello and to stroke and pat her.

"Oooh, I DO like this new life with my Daddy! Everyone seems to love me. This is great!"

OK, Scally was a new member of the office family, but everyone we met seemed to love her and I think she felt that and responded in kind – in spite of her earlier experience. As she matured, she became more and more affectionate and trusting, something that worried me in case anyone tried to steal her. However, for the moment I was simply delighted she was so happy!

While the Scally love-in was going on, I read and signed several reports, printed off the photographs I had taken of that day's rectory survey and collected fresh batteries for my dictaphone and camera. We then headed for home.

The first thing to do, upon arrival back in Wincanton, was to take Scally for her evening walk. By this time, it was dark although the town was lit up with streetlights. There was a light drizzle falling, so I put Scally's coat on her and we set out.

She had had so much exercise at lunchtime I decided on just a short walk. This took us up the High Street a little way then a left turn, up a steep side street to the top, another left turn along a (now unlit) path between stone walls, over a stile and into the "cow-field" of yesterday. Thankfully, there was no sign of the cows this time, as we proceeded across the nearest top part of the field, over another stile and back into the picnic park area above our car park beside the flats. It took little more than a quarter of an hour, but Scally did all her business, bless her.

It was a popular walk, given the number of times Scally stopped to sniff the scents of other dogs and to leave her "calling-card". It became a regular end-of-the-day walk for us – particularly during the dark winter evenings after work.

Collecting my briefcase from the car, we entered the front door of the flats. There were several residents in the main hall and nearly all made a great fuss of the latest "resident".

"Oh, MORE lovely people! Everyone is SO nice to me. I'm beginning to feel this is really my home now!"

I thanked my lucky stars we had just been for a walk and hopefully, Scally's bladder was now well and truly empty. I would *not* have been popular if she had widdled on anybody's foot!

Scally showed just a little hesitation to enter the lift, which surprised me. Perhaps she did not want to say goodbye to her welcoming delegation of elderly residents – her new fan club!

Back in the flat I fed her, changed into jeans and a sweater, poured myself a drink and started to think about supper.

I had an L-shaped sofa, such that at one end it extended out so that you could sit comfortably with your legs up. I had put a sheepskin mat on this for Scally, as her basket was still in my bedroom. She grew to like sitting on it, so that she could see me in the kitchen and could also look out of the window – from the same position.

It was one of the reasons my brother Mark and I had chosen this flat for our late mother. It was on the top floor with a lift and the sitting room was double aspect. The windows faced west over the car park and the town's rooftops beyond, and north over the little park nearby. These made the room light and airy, also giving it interesting views for our mother to enjoy. And now it was Scally's turn!

Tonight, with the drizzle falling and the yellow streetlights illuminating the cars in the car park below, the trees dividing it from the road and reflecting off the wet road itself – it created almost a Christmas scene, but without the snow.

Scally was fascinated, watching the shoppers go to and fro from their cars to the adjacent Co-op supermarket and back again. I was pleased that she was so interested in things around her – and she remained inquisitive throughout her life.

After supper (which tonight I managed to finish before it was stolen), I watched some television and relaxed – with Scally stretched out beside me, her head in my lap, as I stroked her soft silky ears and tickled her chest. Every now and then, she let out a groan of pleasure.

"Ooooh, this is PERFECT! Nobody has ever done this for me. I'm really beginning to feel safe with this lovely man!"

After her recent experience of being lost, cold, hungry and frightened – then being kept at Miss Athill's place in pretty rough conditions with a lot of other dogs – Scally must have been thinking she'd died and gone to heaven!

As for me, she was proving to be a very affectionate and easy companion and I already felt great tenderness towards her as well as protectiveness. I had undoubtedly spent much of the past two and a half days thinking and worrying about her, trying to anticipate her every need and making her feel loved – and this was how I devoted each day to her, thereafter.

I know it sounds corny, but that is what you do when you have a dog. He or she has always to come first.

I watched the national and international news – not nearly as exciting or as life-changing as my recent change of circumstances – and then took Scally down in the lift for her last penny. There were none of her earlier hesitations about entering the lift and I felt some relief that we appeared to have cracked that particular nut.

Disappointingly for Scally, all the other residents had gone to bed and the reception hall was deserted.

I had to be pretty careful about not locking us out. For security reasons the main door always closed automatically behind anyone leaving the building and then locked itself – so I had taken the precaution of wearing, under my shirt, the main door key on a long string around my neck. Robert Baden-Powell would have been *very* proud of me!

Business concluded, Scally and I went back inside out of the rain and upstairs to bed.

***

Next morning, we followed the same routine and I was conscious of being inspected by more than one resident as I stood there in my dressing gown and slippers, waiting for Scally to perform.

After breakfast and Scally's morning walk, I sat down at my table to complete my survey report on the rectory.

I had telephoned my client purchaser yesterday evening to let him know how I had got on, what the main defects were and whether – in my opinion – he needed to be unduly concerned by any of them.

In this respect, I often had to explain that many defects are common to most, if not all, houses of this age and type. For example, usually such period properties have suffered at least some rising damp in the walls for hundreds of years, but it rarely affects the structural integrity of a building to any significant degree.

In most cases, such damp has already been alleviated by various methods, but it often re-appears from time to time, usually just here and there and can normally be rectified fairly easily on an ad hoc basis. It therefore can and should be regarded as a maintenance issue, and part and parcel of owning an old property.

The point is, I did not want to be the cause of sales falling through.

There was no conflict of interest on my part. However, I was frequently recommended by the estate agents selling the property to intending purchasers as being an experienced surveyor who would give them a balanced opinion. I did not want such client purchasers taking fright and pulling out of deals unnecessarily leading to my getting the reputation of being "heavy-handed", in turn resulting in my work drying up.

So, clients needed that perspective – that balanced opinion in order to recognise the condition of their intended property *was acceptable in relation to its age.*

That said, if there *was* a genuine cause for concern, of course, this had to be spelt out. Often, I identified serious structural issues or maybe the need for a complete new private drainage system, rewiring or other such potentially expensive defects – requiring costly remedial works. I told the clients, but I tended to forewarn the estate agents as well – in the interests of preserving my good name and assisting with any renegotiation of the sale price.

Scally had snoozed quietly throughout this conversation.

She was proving to be remarkably undemanding save for affection, which was understandable. I thought that she was probably pretty tired out still, after her rescue from Birmingham and the dreadful drive home, after her games with William yesterday in the stable yard and – yes – now the stress of finding herself in entirely new surroundings and being looked after by a stranger – could he be trusted?

I was glad to say that I was fairly sure her last concern was fading fast.

So, I spent the morning dictating my rectory survey report, at least the remainder of it. I had managed to dictate parts during the survey.

Dee called me twice with details of potential clients seeking quotes for surveys. We recognised it was essential to reply to these enquiries as soon as possible to try to win the instruction from our competitors and each call took about 15 minutes – by the time I had established the age and size of the property and its distance away… in other words how long the job was likely to take me.

Scally was quiet to start with, looking out of the window at the comings and goings below but became rather bored and restive towards lunchtime. I could not blame her – so was I!

I put my coat on, likewise Scally's coat on her, collected together my paperwork, put it in my briefcase and then we headed for the lift.

Much to Scally's delight, our House Manager was in her little office by the main door chatting to a couple of residents. They made an enormous fuss of Scally whose bottom was wagging from side to side along with her tail!

"Oooh, hello everyone! I've had SUCH a boring morning waiting for my Daddy to finish droning away into a little black box. It's SO lovely to see you. Thank you for being so nice to me!"

My heart was in my mouth. Would she widdle with excitement? My hand closed over the paper kitchen towels in my pocket in readiness as I remembered that when we last went out it was 09:30 – three hours ago. She didn't disgrace me – and I loved her the more for it!

After a brief lunchtime walk, we set off for the office.

Scally was now hopping into her cage, inside the car, without hesitation – and I think she quite liked it. Perhaps she felt safer and more secure, maybe the car sickness was no longer a problem for her – but either way, I no longer had to bribe her into it with little treats.

Having loaded her in, I quickly visited the nearby Co-op to get a sandwich for my lunch and ate it whilst driving (ever so slowly) over to Gillingham.

Scally never took her eyes off me as I ate, ears pricked like handlebars, in the hope I might give her a morsel. I did so, making a future rod for my own back. Keeping my eyes on the road, I pushed it through the bars of her cage, just behind me and felt her soft muzzle taking it gently from my fingers.

"Mmm! That's nice. Why does your food taste so much nicer than mine? Any more going? You still have another sandwich on the dashboard waiting to be eaten. Don't forget me, back here!"

That little gesture became another lifetime ritual and if I forgot to give her a little bit of what I was eating and swallowed the lot – there would be an aggrieved whine of disappointment from behind me!

Back in Gillingham, Scally stood on her hind legs, front legs on Dees' lap, whilst the two of them had a love-in. I had to search through the paperwork on Dees' desk myself for the message book, as she had her hands full of my dog and was not to be interrupted!

Dear old Toby, under her desk, took it all in his stride – *what* a gentleman he was! When Toby had first arrived in the office as a rescue dog, he was a little nervous. So Dee put a notice on our department door which read "Caution! New nervous dog in training. Please don't stroke him". I had added a note underneath "…and the same applies to the surveyor!".

I had several telephone calls to return, reports to check through and sign and details of tomorrow's survey to investigate.

Dee or Ann always downloaded the selling agents' sales details – in particular, directions to find the property and floor plans to help me during the survey itself.

It was good to spend just a few minutes confirming my route to the property – and checking the floor plans in anticipation of any internal support issues. It was also useful to find out the nature of the sub-soil from the geological survey map on my office wall and to print off a copy of the Listing details – if the property was listed as being of historic or architectural importance.

I once surveyed a listed house down near Bridport that had been significantly altered internally. It looked nothing like the original description in the Listing Notice, similarly important period features specifically mentioned in the listing were missing – and I had to double-check that I was surveying the correct property! Not only that, but subsequently we could find no Listed Building Consents for the alterations.

My client could have found himself under a legal obligation to restore the interior using period building methods, had he bought the property – which would have cost him a fortune.

Scally meanwhile had joined me in my back office. She climbed into her "office" bed under my side table and found the chew I had left there for her (and work resumed in Dees' office next door!).

All jobs finally done, Scally and I said our good-byes, put our heads around the door of the main front office – to say "Hi" and "Good-bye" – and headed for the office car park. Like I said, I spent more time out of the office than in it and I did not want people to forget what I looked like! It was almost going-home time anyway. The (slow) drive home was uneventful, we did another "town" walk to allow Scally to stretch her legs and do her business and then went in, up to the flat.

We spent a similar evening to the day before, cuddled up on the sofa after supper and then headed for bed, following a quick excursion outside for Scally's benefit.

These were typical workdays for Scally and I, and she always accompanied me.

Winter, spring and autumn days were easier to deal with from the point of view of the weather.

It was the really hot summer days that always worried me. I could not leave Scally in the car parked in the sun. It became like an oven and so I had to find ways around the problem.

If I was lucky, I could get the car under cover if there was a garage free or a barn. Then I would leave her in the car – in her cage and with the windows down – but always checked her on a regular basis.

I could occasionally get the car under some trees in the shade, but as the sun moved around, I would need to move the car as well.

Sometimes I had to shut Scally in a stable or in an empty outbuilding – and failing that occasionally I even tied her to a tree providing effective shade.

The first time I did this I suddenly found Scally's face beside mine about half an hour later, licking my ear as I was on my hands and knees peering under an upstairs floorboard. She had chewed through the rope I had used to tie her to the tree and had then followed my scent to find me!

"Hello, Daddy! What are you looking at down there? Is it something nice to eat?! Sorry, I got bored, tied to a tree, so I thought I would come and see what you're doing. Can I help you?"

After that, I used a chain, which proved totally effective from my point of view, totally frustrating from Scally's!

Occasionally the house to be surveyed was empty and in hot conditions, I brought Scally's bed into the house, where she eventually settled down for a snooze – after first wandering around the unfurnished rooms, exploring.

I had not factored in the problem of increasingly hot summers when I was considering getting a dog all those months ago.

Another problem was fireworks.

People have an *infuriating* habit of letting off fireworks more or less a week either side of November 5th. Unfortunately, the same applies if Aunt Agatha or any other member of the family is having a birthday, on anniversaries, on New Years' Eve – and at any other time that even the feeblest excuse can be found to celebrate something.

What people do not stop to consider are the frightening, sometimes terrifying, effects that fireworks have on animals, both domestic and wild – not to mention farm animals.

Disaster struck on November 2nd, about 10 months after I rescued Scally, when we were enjoying our evening walk together through the field close to the car park and parkland adjoining our block of flats. We had just reached the ridge when a rocket shot up into the darkness from somewhere below and exploded with an almost ear-splitting *BANG*, followed by another, then another.

Scally stood stock still, more surprised than frightened and as there were no further fireworks, she tentatively moved forward – now on her lead.

"Oh, my goodness, WHAT was that? I've never heard THAT before… oh well, my master doesn't seem too worried. Perhaps there's nothing to worry about."

We had almost completed our walk when there was another salvo of explosions, bright lights and bangs. This was too much for Scally.

"Oh NO! Someone's trying to kill us! We've got to run for our lives! Come on, Master, COME ON! DON'T HANG AROUND, THEY'LL GET US!"

My frightened dog tried to make a run for it, back to our flat.

From then on and throughout her life, Scally was *terrified* of fireworks. It was heart-breaking to see her shaking with fright, eyes wide and panting – with her pink tongue lolling out, dripping saliva.

I consulted the vet who sold me a plug-in medical odouriser to calm her, also a calming spray which I applied to her collar and to her bed. These worked quite well, but as you never quite knew when they would be needed, my poor girl used to shake with fright for 20 minutes until the treatment took effect.

In such circumstances, it was better to behave entirely normally – as if there was no problem. Greatly tempted though I was to cuddle and soothe her, it only seemed to make her more anxious.

I cannot think why legislation has not been enacted to make the use of fireworks subject to lawful control – such as having to obtain a local authority licence by confirming a "qualifying occasion" and their use by a responsible adult.

I am not a spoilsport nor narrow-minded. But if you keep finding yourself having to comfort a much loved, terrified animal when the situation could be avoided, you too might reconsider the unregulated use of fireworks.

Thunder and lightning had the same effect on Scally. Fortunately, it never occurred during one of my surveys, which would have been promptly interrupted and quite possibly abandoned!

Part Three

Our Weekends

Until I was due to retire in 2015, three years ahead, virtually every weekend was spent on the boat and thereafter a lot *more* time!

So – at the end of that very first week together, late on Friday afternoon 20th January 2012, just four days after Scally's collection from Birmingham, we set off for my narrow boat "Bluebell" – moored at the bottom of a farmer's field bordering the Kennet & Avon Canal near Hilperton, on the edge of Trowbridge.

By the time we reached the little car park serving our moorings, it was 6:30 p.m. – and pitch dark at that time of year.

Bluebell was almost the furthest boat in the line of boats moored alongside the canal – located perhaps 500 yards away.

There was one wheelbarrow (our only mooring facility) shared with about 30 other boats and I was grateful to see it sitting there.

I piled as much as I could fit into the wheelbarrow including Scally's bean bag, her food, my food for the weekend and a bag of spare clothes in case I fell in! With Scally on her lead, we tramped along by torchlight until we reached Bluebell. Leaving Scally attached to the wheelbarrow I unlocked the boats' aft doors and unloaded everything onto my bed.

We returned to the car for our second load of 2 x 5 litre canisters of drinking water, a bag of smokeless coal and two bags of logs. Scally trotted along obligingly beside me, stopping every now and then to sniff an interesting scent, which she usually then smothered with a penny.

After our second off-load onto Bluebell we returned the wheelbarrow to the car park, for anyone else to use, perhaps arriving later.

"This is a weird sort of walk, Master. Backwards and forwards, backwards and forwards! How many more times…?!"

By the time we reached my boat a third time, it was starting to drizzle, and we had walked some 2500 yards – quite far enough for Scally's evening walk, multiple pennies and more serious business (collected!).

I had already learned *not* to mistakenly leave anything in the car that I might need later!

Bluebell was served by a small wooden landing stage giving access to the back of the boat. By torchlight, I encouraged Scally to step from the safety of the landing stage onto Bluebell's stern – which was only about six inches out from the landing stage and at the same level.

"You MUST be joking, Master! Look, there's water down there. I might fall in! You go first and show me."

Scally was *not* keen, so I stepped across the narrow gap onto the stern to show her it was safe and, bless her, she tentatively followed.

"Oh, OK. So, you think if you do it, then I will? Well, I don't fancy hanging around out here in the rain all night and I'm hungry – I want my dinner! So, I'll give it a go, but be ready to catch me, OK?"

Next, there were a couple of deep steps down into the back of the boat, before entering the living quarters.

"Now where are you taking me?"

Again, rather nervously she followed me down into the bedroom – and then spotting the bed, she hopped up onto my duvet with alacrity, amongst all the bags!

"YAY! A lovely big soft bed. Maybe Master hasn't lost his marbles, after all!"

I switched on the batteries for the electrical supply, turned on the lights, then wiped Scally's paws and dried her off generally. My next job was to start the engine – to charge up the batteries and to heat the water. I then lit the wood-burning stove in the front of the boat – to dry out the cold and slightly damp atmosphere and to generate some serious heat!

I was still learning the most effective way of getting a fire started and keeping it alight. Tonight, I adjusted the draught beneath the stove, laid the fire carefully and then put a match to it.

Within just a minute or two, there was a satisfactory golden glow through the front glass as the flames spread from the firelighters to ignite the kindling and logs, leaping upwards and providing much welcome warmth.

I unloaded the food bags, storing perishables in the fridge and Scally's food in one of the kitchen cupboards. I put my spare clothes away, found a place to put Scally's bean bag and transferred the coal and the logs from the stern into the engine room, also rescuing the two canisters of water, storing them in the kitchen.

Getting aboard and storing everything away was a necessary chore, but a prelude to then relaxing with a glass of whisky in front of the fire and the enjoyment of planning and anticipating the weekend ahead.

Whilst all this was going on, Scally had helpfully remained out of the way on my bed on my duvet (or was possibly under it by now!). I made her supper and called her through to the front sitting room area, where there was space for her food and water bowls. After a moment or two, she came trotting through, wagging her tail – and tucked in.

"Oh THANKS, Master. I'm famished! My tummy's been grumbling for hours. I could eat ALL that food you brought for the weekend right now, all at once!"

I poured myself a drink and relaxed in front of the glowing stove.

I looked around the front cabin, savouring being back on board and the feeling of cosiness – of being home again. Whilst the flat provided our accommodation during the week and in fairness it was a lovely flat with great views, it was my

62

sister's and would have to be sold. It was not *my* permanent home.

I had always been brought up to regard one's home as perhaps one's greatest investment and had worked hard for over 40 years to pay the mortgage and to carry out improvements on my townhouse. I had lost all that in the recent recession and now I had replaced it with a canal boat.

Did I mind?

Well, I would not have planned it this way – but actually – I was now enjoying myself more than at any time I could remember!

Scally interrupted my musings with a "woof", wagging her tail and looking expectantly at the L-shaped dinette I was sitting on – the boat's equivalent of a sofa.

"Ooh, this is nice and cosy… and NICE FIRE!! But I want to sit beside you to feel its heat."

She was asking to come up with me rather than slum it on her bean bag!

She got a rather nasty shock when instead I took her outside and walked her a hundred yards down the moorings in the drizzle, to spend a penny.

"Hey, is this REALLY necessary? I'm going to get all wet again and I spent hundreds of pennies earlier on our "marathon" walk."

She always seemed to need to do a penny after being fed… and she duly obliged this time.

Upon our return to Bluebell, she was a lot happier jumping off the landing stage onto the stern, than she was earlier jumping off the stern onto the landing stage. Her wish to get back on board, out of the drizzle and into the warmth of the cabin was proving to be a good training incentive!

Having dried her and wiped her paws again (and put the duvet back on my bed) I once more settled down on the dinette – Scally beside me on a sheepskin, her head in my lap.

Oooh, this is SO nice! A full tummy, a warm fire and cuddling up to my master!

The size of the boat meant that we would be living at closer quarters with one another than in the flat and in turn, this probably meant allowing Scally more liberties. What the hell! I didn't mind. In fact, I quite liked the companionship – but I would keep the bean bag handy as a place for her to dry out in front of the fire if she came in really wet.

The fire had started to die down, so I reduced the draught a little and fed it three more logs and a couple of bits of coal – to keep it happy for another hour or so.

From the open foredeck in the bows, which was fitted with painted steel seats on either side, part glazed hardwood double front doors gave access to storage steps just inside the boat, leading down into the open-plan front cabin.

This consisted of our sitting room area, with the kitchen behind/beyond.

Our sitting room contained the wood-burning stove on one side of the entrance doors and a shelved storage unit on the other, incorporating a TV. Further into the cabin was the L-shaped dinette with a huge amount of storage space beneath and two recesses in the floor for struts to support quite a large tabletop. Shorter struts were available to lower the tabletop within the angle of the dinette so that using the cushions – a double bed for visitors was created in front of the wood-burner – cosy!

The kitchen was "U"-shaped, adjoining the inner end of the dinette and was well equipped with work surfaces and with a full-sized gas oven with four hobs, a stainless-steel sink and drainer, a full-sized 12-volt fridge and plenty of cupboard and shelving space.

The boat was only 6ft 10ins wide and of the 45ft overall length the sitting room area and kitchen probably accounted for just 18 ft. Nonetheless, this main cabin felt spacious yet cosy.

From the back of the kitchen, there was a door into a narrow passageway on one side, leading past a small bathroom. This contained a shower above a hip bath, a circular washbasin and a WC. In order to conserve water, I only ever used the shower (the water storage tank was in the bows) and the contents of the WC went into a holding tank which needed to be pumped out now and then.

Moving along the passageway and beyond the bathroom, was my bedroom – equipped with a small 4ft wide double bed with wall mounted cupboards above at one end and a fitted double wardrobe at the other. The hot water cylinder lay on its side on the floor of this wardrobe, keeping my clothes warm and dry. Beneath the bed were two enormously deep storage drawers, guaranteed to swallow up all sorts of things – never to be seen again.

An internal door opened from my bedroom to steps up into the "engine room", so called because the engine was located beneath the floor. There were double steel doors from here and a sliding hatch above, all giving access out onto the open stern at the back of the boat.

This engine room was effectively my back lobby, also known as my "garden shed", as it was a great place to store my tools, mooring pins and mallet, muddy boots and all sorts of other detritus associated with keeping a boat. (Damp coats were hung close to the wood-burning stove in the front cabin).

Within the main living areas, the walls were lined in ash panelling, beneath a beautiful pine-clad ceiling. On bright summer days the sunlight dancing on the surface of the water outside reflected onto this ceiling in what I imagined to be "arrowheads" of living white light.

When I had bought Bluebell, the flooring was covered part in worn wood laminate or otherwise old carpet. I had since replaced these with large cream and brown vinyl tiles, laid down the length of the boat in a diamond pattern. These proved to be more practical for cleaning and looked really striking.

At the same time, I had the lower wall panelling covered in white tongue and groove boarding, lightening up the interior, but retaining the boat's essential character.

This was to be Scally's future home, as well as mine – and she had made herself remarkably comfortable already!

Having gone out through the front double doors and opened the foredeck hatch to the gas locker, I turned on the gas and returned inside to cook my supper – to the accompaniment of occasional groans of bliss from Scally – lying on the dinette in front of the warm fire.

Why had I been so worried about her adapting to all the new changes in her life? She was evidently a great deal more adaptable than I had given her credit for!

That said, I knew I must protect her as well. She was not much more than a puppy still and not entirely used to her new life yet – and certainly not to the pitfalls of living on a narrow boat on a canal.

I opened a bottle of red wine to celebrate the joy of being back on board and savoured a glass with my meal of spaghetti bolognese sprinkled with parmesan cheese.

I ate this – having erected the dinette table – watching telly and marvelled at the home comforts of narrow boat living! A lovely warm fire, one of my favourite meals with a glass of wine, TV and a doggy companion. I almost groaned in bliss as well!

All the while the engine had been rumbling away in the back of the boat. It had long gone 8 p.m., the time generally accepted by canal boaters after which engines should not be run. I went back to the engine room and turned it off.

Upon my return, there was my plate upside down on the floor, knife and fork scattered some distance away – and my companion looking at me from her bean bag, licking her lips and looking immensely satisfied.

"Ooh, that was SO good! Thank you, Master!"

I'd been had... again!

I feigned being seriously displeased without frightening her but as before, I only had myself to blame. She had made such a fuss as she sat beside me on the dinette as I ate my supper, I had banished her to her bean bag – and now she had got her own back!

I washed up (now there was plenty of hot water) and then watched the 10 o'clock news to keep myself up to date with world events – remarkably few, that evening.

After that, it was time to give Scally her final run before turning in. She was not too keen to leave the warmth of the cabin, but the rain had stopped, the clouds had cleared, and it was a starry night. She baulked again at stepping off the boat onto the landing stage, but it was only a momentary hesitation this time.

We were back on board within five minutes, all business concluded.

"Come on, Master! Don't hang around. Let's get back on the boat. It's so warm and comfy in there!"

Scally had fairly dragged me, on the end of her lead, back onto the boat without any hesitation this time and down below. She could not wait to get back to the wood-burning stove. Single-minded, or what?!

I put some coals onto the fire, reduced the draught to almost nothing and closed the front of the stove. The coals would be slower burning, so that the stove should remain alight all night, just giving off a comfortable heat.

Once washed and in my pyjamas, I left Scally on her sheepskin on the dinette in the front cabin, enjoying the heat of the fire – and headed aft to bed. I was a little concerned about leaving Scally rather close to the hot outer casing of the stove. However, I had tested the smoke and carbon monoxide alarms when I came aboard, I would be reading for a while, and I was a light sleeper.

I put the light out after an hour or so, reflecting that our first evening together on the boat had gone well – even taking into account the plate incident – and fell asleep.

Next morning, I awoke to find a furry hot water bottle cuddled up to me. Perhaps I was not such a light sleeper after all. I had absolutely no recollection of Scally creeping in under the duvet during the night.

I had decided to spend a quiet weekend on the boat without going anywhere – to give Scally a chance to get used to living aboard. After all, we had only been together for little over four days and her world must have seemed like a confusing kaleidoscope of sudden changes.

Remarkably so far, she seemed to have taken her new life in her stride, but I realised *I* was the constant in each of those changes and I needed to give her more of my undivided attention during our early days together, to build up her confidence.

So, I was in no rush to get up, save to start the engine (for more hot water), for a visit to the bathroom and to make myself a mug of coffee. The wood-burner had "stayed in", with just a small red glow remaining, providing comfortable warmth in the front cabin.

When I returned to bed, Scally decided she was too hot where she was. She climbed out from under the head of the duvet, turned around and flopped down on top of it, facing away from me, her back legs flat out behind her pointing towards me and giving me the full benefit of her bottom. Doubtless this was to cool her tummy and was a habit of hers throughout her life.

I hauled her around so that I could stroke her head and her ears, telling her what a lovely girl she was and how clever to cope with all these changes in her young life.

I do not suppose for a moment she understood a word of what I was saying but I think she liked the tone of my voice. She wagged her tail, gave me a lick and with a groan of pleasure turned over onto her back with all four legs in the air – clearly inviting me to tickle her tummy.

Go for it, Master! I'm loving all this attention. I've never been so well cared for!

It seemed she was not short on confidence – nor modesty – after all!

After I had finished my coffee and after our start-of-the-day love-in, I climbed out of bed and headed into the sitting room. I removed the tray of warm ash from beneath the firebox of the stove, unlocked the front outer doors, stepped out into the bows and – first checking the wind direction – carefully tipped the ash into a tin bucket, put there for the purpose.

Tipping anything into the canal was frowned upon, but I had no landing stage at the front of the boat – and I certainly was not going to carry hot ash all the way through the boat. So, the bucket served as my onboard disposal facility for ash from the stove, until I was going ashore.

Retreating back inside, I then re-laid the fire with a little newspaper, kindling, logs and a couple of pieces of coal.

Increasing the draught a little, I watched the fire come to life and almost immediately felt the warmth building again in the front cabin.

That done, I pulled on a dressing gown and a pair of workman's waterproof boots, collected Scally and we then ventured outside through the engine room and out onto the stern. Scally barely hesitated as she stepped across the narrow gap and onto the landing stage.

She would get a proper walk later, but this was just to give her the opportunity to do her early morning business ashore and not on the boat – although in fairness we had not had any such mishaps in the flat to date. It seemed that provided I anticipated Scally's requirements, she was pretty well fully house trained.

It was a cold, bright morning after yesterday's drizzle, thin sunshine trying to break through the freezing early morning fog, blue sky and high cirrus cloud visible above – and the grass was white with frost. Smoke from my stubby chimney, projecting through the roof of Bluebell, curled upwards into the still morning air. My favourite winter weather conditions – a truly beautiful day! A good omen!

We were at the bottom of the farmers field, walking along a mown grassed pathway, crisp underfoot with frost and bordered by boats moored beside the canal – of different lengths and painted a variety of colour schemes. Those that were occupied mostly had smoke coming from their chimneys, like Bluebells.

It is a well-known fact that dogs seem to find mooring pins the most tempting objects to pee over, and this is *highly* unpopular with boaters – who then have to handle their mooring lines before casting off.

Scally was no exception. However, she was on her lead and so I was able to discourage her from getting too close and committing the heinous sin of watering my neighbours' property.

We only needed to walk a hundred yards or so before our mission was completed. On turning around and heading back to the boat, Scally set off like a bolting horse, evidently keen to get back to the warmth on board and to have her breakfast.

"OH YESSS! Quick, let's get back to the boat. I'm starving!"

I was interested to see if she knew which boat was ours.

I was not disappointed. She unerringly turned off the path when we reached Bluebell and hopped off the landing stage and onto the stern, nose against the outer back doors, tail wagging and looking back at me. I could swear she was smiling!

I was delighted! It meant that if for some reason I lost her near the boats, she would hopefully know her way back to *our* boat.

Back down below I fed Scally and then went through my morning routine of getting washed, shaved, dressed, made the bed and turned off the engine. I tickled up the kettle again, made myself another mug of coffee and ate a bowl of cereal – livened up with a chopped banana and sliced grapes.

I then tidied up, put another couple of logs on the fire, erected the table and got out the survey files that I had brought. Scally meanwhile had reclaimed her poll position on her sheepskin on the dinette, warming herself in front of the stove – now with her head on my lap, bean bag discarded.

73

I settled down to some serious reading. I quite liked checking reports – seeing the results of my labours in print accompanied by numerous explanatory photographs. However, such reports needed to be carefully written, unambiguous and just as carefully checked for accuracy.

It was a lot easier to scrutinise them aboard the boat in peace and quiet without any stress or interruptions – than it was in the office with calls to be answered, or at home in the evening when I was usually tired and found it more difficult to concentrate.

I checked through a couple of reports which took almost three hours, then turned my attention to lunch – nearly always a light snack, when I was aboard. I was usually busy during the day, whereas I could better relax and enjoy a more substantial meal in the evening.

Scally was due for a proper walk, so once I had finished eating, I put on my coat and pulled on my boots, and we set off.

From our moorings, it was possible to walk east alongside the canal through the adjacent fields to an old brick bridge about half a mile away. This spanned the canal so that crossing over and turning west, one was on the main towpath then heading back towards our private car park. Here there was another little bridge which gave us access back over the canal once more and into the farmer's field and to our moorings.

It was a nice "round" of a walk and Scally was enjoying herself. I had her on an extendable lead to give her as much freedom as possible – but longed to let her off it altogether. However, we had barely been together five days yet and I would just have to be patient.

She found masses of interesting scents, stopping and sniffing and often leaving her "mark". Clearly, there was a lot of wildlife around, including rabbits and perhaps badgers.

She pushed her head into a large hole with fresh earth dug out in front of it, perhaps originally an entrance to a badgers' set – although there were fresh rabbit droppings in front of it now.

She was also fascinated by the moorhens, the ducks and the swans on the canal. I do not think she had ever met a swan before, barking aggressively at a couple as they glided over to see if I had any food for them. In all the years we were on the canal she never got used to them, always barking and seemingly daring them to chase her.

We also came face to face with a heron, a very tall, long-legged and elegant grey skinny bird with contrasting dark wings and a long beak. He had a long neck too, decorated by a thin double line of black feathers down the front.

The bird reminded me of one of my tutors – a tall, emaciated school master wearing his gown and the school tie.

It stood quite still on the canal bank so that I wondered for a moment whether it was a statue that had been placed there. Then the heron took off and flew up the canal, resembling a pre-historic pterodactyl in flight.

A variety of narrow boats motored slowly past, mainly "liveaboards" with all sorts of interesting detritus stored on their roofs – including logs, bags of coal, bicycles and carrier-trailers, gas bottles, children's tricycles, tin baths, the odd armchair, water carriers, the occasional statue, maybe a canoe and often solar panels to charge their boat batteries.

I always waved and they were happy to wave back.

They represent a community who have chosen to live closer to nature and to the environment around us, for the most part, big-hearted people, *always* ready to help another boater in trouble. A really nice crowd with deep-seated convictions and without whom the canal would be a lesser place in respect of both kindness and character.

Every now and then, as we walked along, we would hear a bicycle bell behind us, and we then stood aside to let usually two or three bicyclists go past. At this time of year, the towpath was worn with muddy puddles in places – and the "cool" absence of mudguards always amused me, resulting in a line of wet mud up the cyclists' bottom, back and helmet… I really could *not* see the point!

We passed just a small number of boats moored on this side of the canal, some clearly locked up – others occupied with smoke curling upwards from their stove-pipe chimneys. However, we saw no one to stop and talk to. There was also an interesting view of our line of boats, moored on the other side of the canal.

Having reached our little car park and crossed over the canal by way of the farmer's brick bridge, we were back to our line of moorings – where a few of my neighbouring boaters were out and about.

There is always the odd job needing to be done on a narrowboat even at this time of year – whether it be emptying the ash pan and bringing in more coal and logs, or tacking wire netting to a wooden landing stage, to stop it becoming lethally slippery. With the icy and frosty conditions of this morning, I was thankful that I had taken that precaution about a month ago.

People had got to know me without a dog – so there was much interest in my new four-legged companion.

Scally was greatly admired and enjoyed the fuss being made of her. She was very much a "people" dog, in spite of having experienced the cruelty of being dumped only a matter of a few months before. I loved her for her innocent trust, but also realised, as earlier, that she would need to be protected from it. I did not want her to be stolen.

She was doing her utmost to escape... by straining on the end of her lead in order to hop onto the nearest boat! Whether she was motivated by the kind lady making a fuss of her, or the exciting scent of a roast dinner aboard, I could not tell – but I could guess!

"Oh Master, PLEASE let me go! I can smell something really good on this boat. It's making my mouth water and I'm SO hungry again! PLEASE, just for a moment..."

This little walk back to our boat took nearly half an hour – given the explanations and chatting along the way – and daylight was fading as we negotiated our landing stage, then stepped onto the stern of Bluebell.

After unlocking the aft doors, I towelled Scally down in the engine room, before letting her into the cabin – insisting she dried off on her bean bag. She was not keen on that idea, but *no way* was I going to put up with still damp and dirty paws on my duvet or on her sheepskin.

The boat remained warm but there was only the tiniest glow from the stove, indicating it needed "feeding" again.

Opening the bow doors, I topped up the coalscuttle from the bag I had brought with us – now stored under one bow seat – and brought in an armful of logs from beneath the other seat. Some of the logs were a little damp and these I stacked closest to the stove, also on two little metal trivets on top of the stove itself.

Removing the top of one of my entry steps, I grabbed some warm dry kindling from within the hidden storage space beneath, laying it on top of the dying coals in the stove and followed it up with a few fresh coals and three logs, finally shutting the front of the stove and opening the draught a little to get everything well alight.

It only took a moment or two for the kindling to catch and within a couple of minutes, the fire was roaring away – until I reduced the draught.

I reflected that a wood-burning stove is a bit like a two-year-old child in some respects. It needs feeding regularly and constant attention if it is going to behave as desired. After some 20 minutes, the fire was well established – the two-year-old was once more content!

Scally appreciated it, anyway! Her bean bag was on the floor in front of the stove, but now dry she lay – with her cuddly toy rabbit – on her sheepskin, on the dinette, in front of the stove, fast asleep.

She was tired out after our walk and doubtless after her introduction to the boat. It was easy to underestimate all these changes she was having to get used to and I would need to take things quietly, to start with.

I would let her sleep for a while before feeding her and taking her outside for a penny.

By now it was just after 4 p.m., virtually dark outside and I settled down to check the last of the survey reports.

An idea had been germinating in my mind during our walk, earlier. Much as I loved simply being aboard the boat, I knew I would be bored tomorrow if we did not do something a little different.

We were getting rather low on water, also on fuel and our nearest boatyard was only 20 minutes steaming time up the canal – a nice short trip to gently introduce Scally to the joys of cruising.

Hang on a minute, WHAT was I thinking!? Only two minutes ago, I realised I was possibly under-estimating all the changes that Scally was having to get used to aboard the boat, telling myself I needed to take things quietly to start with – and now here I was, about to ignore all my good intentions of a quiet first weekend aboard, on our mooring… and was thinking of taking her cruising instead!

In the end, I decided – let's see what the weather is like tomorrow. If it is a horrible wet windy day, we'll stay put where we are, warm and snug and the decision would have been made for us. But if it is another bright day like today and after Scally's had a good night's sleep, maybe we'll give it a go.

What I wanted to avoid was a trip up to the boatyard the following weekend, when supplies would be even lower and perhaps in the pouring rain. And if it turned out to be windy too, controlling a 45ft narrowboat broadside onto the wind is well-nigh impossible.

Oh well, all would be revealed in the morning!

Meanwhile, I had the survey report to check through. There would not be time to read it in the morning if we were taking the boat up to the boatyard – and I certainly did not want to have to check it tomorrow evening when we got back to the flat.

The evening progressed very much as before and after finally turning out the light above my bed, I reflected on how well our day together had gone. I had _so_ enjoyed being back on the boat with time to devote to Scally and I could not have asked for a calmer reaction to our new surroundings.

***

On looking out of the porthole beside my bed the next morning, I could see that it was another lovely bright winter's day. Fantastic! Maybe we would do Plan A after all – a short trip up to the boatyard.

I went through to the main cabin and found Scally snoozing peacefully on her beanbag in front of the still-warm stove.

I emptied the ash tray into the bucket as before and fed a couple of logs and some nuggets of coal into the stove – increasing the draught – whilst I waited for the kettle to boil for a mug of coffee.

Scally was in no rush to get up, so after fondling her ears and telling her she was a lovely girl, I took my coffee into the bathroom with me.

Once dressed, I gave Scally her breakfast and whilst she was eating, I put on my nice warm coat (which had been hanging close to the stove all night) and pulled on my boots.

Scally came trotting through to the engine room as I opened up the aft doors and the overhead hatch and we set off down the line of boats for her morning "constitutional".

Her business concluded and upon our return to Bluebell, I considered our first voyage together whilst I ate my breakfast.

There were various preparations to remember to make before setting off :-

- Reduce the draught out through the base of the stove (I had needed to replace the front glass once already – which was cracked by the stove overheating during an earlier trip, given the draught coming *down* the chimney generated as we went along.)
- Adjust the mooring lines, to make it quicker and easier to cast off, when ready.
- Fit the removable brass tiller shaft horizontally into the top of the painted tiller pipe, projecting vertically up through the stern of the boat. This brass shaft is needed to enable effective steering – and many are the times I have forgotten it until the last moment.
- Give the "tap" on top of the brass greaser cylinder a turn – to lubricate the propeller shaft and to stop it over-heating during cruising.
- Check the oil and turn on the fuel.
- Make a flask of coffee to keep me warm when travelling.
- Visit the bathroom before departure! Single-handed cruising is fine until you are caught short – and in the past, I have had to stop the boat midstream provided there are no boats around and rush down to the bathroom.

- Put Scally into her warm coat, put her bean bag in the engine room and attach a safety chain to secure her to the boat. (I had heard terrible stories of both people and dogs falling over the side and being horribly mutilated by the propeller – and without fail, if I had anyone else on board, I always impressed on them the importance of putting the engine into neutral *immediately* if anyone fell over the side. It didn't matter if we lost control of the boat and hit something, it was *far* more important to stop the propeller from turning).

So those were the thoughts going through my mind as I anticipated our first trip together – a bit like an airline pilot's checklist before taking off.

Once I was ready, I started the engine to let it warm up and gave Scally another quick run ashore before we cast off.

Upon our return to Bluebell, I put Scally into her warm coat, fetched her beanbag laying it on the floor of the engine room, and attached her to her safety chain. The chain needed to be just long enough to let her stand with me on the stern and to peer around the rear corner of the upper structure of the boat so that she could see where we were going – yet short enough to prevent her from falling overboard. She also needed to be able to get onto her beanbag if she wanted to.

After some adjustments, I was satisfied and left her to get used to the engine rumbling away beneath her and to my absence whilst I went through my "pre-flight" checks and actions.

"Hey, Master! Don't leave me. I don't like being without you! Come back. Where have you gone?"

She did not like being left, particularly when I went ashore without her to deal with the mooring lines, or whenever I was out of her sight in the boat, and she could not get to me. She barked and whined, but whilst I did not want her becoming distraught, it was something she had to get used to.

I returned to her after a few minutes and made a fuss of her, then left her again whilst I visited the bathroom and waited for the kettle to boil for my flask of coffee.

After about 15 minutes, Scally was beginning to quieten down a little although I could still hear the odd bark – along with a lot of "mutterings" of disgust.

"Come on! Stop faffing about! What are you doing???"

By now I reckoned she would be so relieved I would be standing alongside her once we got underway, that she would not be too worried about being chained to the back of a moving boat.

Well, there was only one way to find out…

It was still a bright sunny morning and I had called the boatyard to make sure they were open and to let them know I was coming. There were no boats approaching – and it was time to cast off.

I let go one end of the bowline, pulling it in from around the front mooring post and coiling it so that it was secure within the bows, then walked back through the boat to cast off the stern line. Again, I coiled this in carefully so that it could not get kicked overboard by mistake. A trailing rope could easily get caught around the propeller just beneath us and would be a nightmare to release – probably needing to be cut away through the weed hatch (giving access to the propeller), whilst the boat drifted and got in people's way.

By now the bows had drifted a little way out into the canal so that Bluebell was in the perfect position for me to simply put her engine into forward gear enabling her to move gently away from the landing stage – having first checked once more that there were no approaching boats.

On the canal and on most other British waterways, we travel as per the continent on the right side of the road – or in this case, on the right side of the canal. Providing everyone knows and respects this – and here I am thinking mostly of hire boaters – it saves a lot of collisions.

I now had a moment to concentrate on Scally, who was standing with her front paws resting right on the very outer edge of the deck, as anticipated peering around the rear corner of the upper superstructure to see where we were going.

She seemed quite relaxed and every now and then would swap sides to get a different view.

"Hey Master, this is fun! Taking our house out onto the water – I've never done this before! There's SO much to look at! I don't want to miss ANYTHING!"

There was not a lot of room on the stern so that she would often push her way between my legs, chain and all. As a result, I was having to regularly extricate myself.

Although her front paws were in a precarious position, the chain would prevent her from falling over the side and indeed she never did lose her footing.

I would have liked to have been able to put her into her life jacket – little more than an outer harness worn over her coat with a handle between her shoulders – so that had she slipped I could have grabbed her and lifted her up– rather like a briefcase! However, the lady in the pet shop had told me it would not be delivered until sometime next week.

After a while Scally got cold, bored, or tired – I was not sure which – and opted to lie down on her beanbag in the engine room.

She liked that! The engine beneath the floor was generating warmth so that her beanbag was warm too and she was sheltered from the cold breeze of our passage. After turning round and round on her beanbag as dogs do (getting herself thoroughly tied up in her chain) she settled down for a snooze. I think the vibration of the engine also relaxed her.

"Mmm, I like this! It's much warmer in here! The floor seems to be alive and very noisy – but Master doesn't seem to be worried, so I won't worry either!"

This gave me a better opportunity to concentrate on where we were going and to avoid colliding with other boats. I also needed to keep a watchful eye out for anything such as baulks of timber or branches floating in the canal which might damage our propeller.

In addition, when passing other boats which are moored, one is expected to slow right down.

The explanation for this lies in the design of the hull. Most canal boats are flat bottomed. Surface tension between the underside of the hull and the water means that a passing boat will be "pulling" water along beneath it. This in turn disturbs the water beneath the nearby moored boat – "pulling" the water beneath it along too. As a result, the moored boat starts to move and its considerable weight can, in turn, pull its mooring pins out of the bank.

The faster the passing boat is going, the greater the "water pull" and the greater the disturbance – *not popular*!

Some of the moored boats we passed were "wide-beams". Whilst a narrow boat is normally 6ft 10ins wide, a wide-beam boat can be 10ft, 12ft or sometimes 14ft wide.

Whilst they are lovely to live on – rather more like living in an apartment on the water – they stick out into the canal taking up more space than a narrow boat and can be rather a nuisance when underway.

Often, when meeting a wide-beam boat coming towards me, I have had to stop Bluebell behind a line of boats on my side to let it past, or to hop ashore with the centre line if there are boats moored alongside the opposite bank.

That said, in my experience wide-beam owners are mostly very considerate and where possible will themselves pull in and wait for other boats to pass. So, it must be something of a nightmare for them too.

Later in Scally's life, my brother, his son and myself hired a wide-beam boat for short holidays on the Thames, a much wider waterway and that was real luxury without the worry of taking up too much space on the water.

There is a bend almost immediately before arriving at the boatyard which lies on the left bank. This was the other side of the canal from me, so I would need to cross the canal, as part of bringing Bluebell alongside the boatyard wharf.

Upon rounding the bend, I could see two boats coming towards me from the opposite direction on the same side as the boatyard and a boat preparing to leave the wharf, which would be heading away from me.

I wondered whether one or both oncoming boats intended stopping at the boatyard, which might involve me in a considerable delay.

Tempting though it was to quickly cross the canal to come in behind the boat just about to leave, the two oncoming boats were on his side of the canal, so he was having to wait for them to go past before he could cast off. There would be insufficient space for both Bluebell and the departing boat alongside the wharf and the two boats coming towards me were perhaps now too close for me to carry out such a manoeuvre without forcing them to take evasive action.

Narrowboats do not have brakes. The only way of slowing down or stopping your boat is to put your engine into reverse but in this case, the oncoming boats would have had to swerve into the centre of the canal to avoid a collision. The owners would have been justifiably disgusted at such unacceptable discourtesy had I tried to cross over in front of them.

These were all considerations that flashed through my mind within literally just a second or two – leading me to the decision to slow right down whilst I waited for the situation to resolve itself… a decision I might say that I had to make with Scally's chain wrapped around my legs, as she was now awake and taking an interest!

One would think that because narrowboats travel slowly, taking such decisions should be easy. However, it is often just the opposite.

It is sometimes difficult to judge a boat's speed if they are heading towards you and should there be an obstruction or a narrowing of the waterway between you – which boat is going to get to the obstruction first? How competent do they seem? Are there boats following along behind them? Do I hang back and let them through first, or crack on to pass the obstruction first? One is constantly taking such decisions on every trip – and the answer is *always* to "drive defensively", usually involving slowing down, until the situation becomes clear.

As it turned out both oncoming boats passed the boatyard without stopping and the boat alongside moved off. After reversing Bluebell back towards the bend to give me space to get into position, I was able to cross the canal and to steer Bluebell towards the wharf.

She is a great boat. She has quite a large propeller and is therefore very responsive to a quick, short, burst of power on the throttle.

So, the trick was to first bring her in *very slowly* at an angle of about 40 degrees, in this case, from the wharf. When her bows were only about 3ft from bumping into it, I pushed the tiller bar hard over to the left/to port – that is, away from me – and gave her a short, meaningful forward burst on the throttle.

This pushed the bows out, bringing the stern in, avoiding any collision with the wharf – and so that we ended up nicely parallel to it. A short burst of throttle in reverse usually slowed her down and brought the stern further in – so that I could step off her onto the wharf, centre line in hand for mooring up.

At least, that was the theory and it usually worked.

All the while I had been keeping an eye on Scally, as I did not want her paws getting crushed between the iron boat and the edge of the concrete wharf.

At the critical moment, as we were coming alongside, I grabbed her chain and pulled her back, saying loudly "Get Back" – and after several trips, I noticed she did not need to be told. She recognised when we were coming alongside, bless her and knew she had to step back from the edge.

Having moored the boat and shut off the engine, I slipped below to check on the stove, leaving Scally chained in position on the stern. She was *not* happy to be left – I could hear her whining – but I also needed to open the front cabin doors to take the hose from the boatman and to remove the water cap so that the tank could be filled. This usually takes at least a quarter of an hour, if not longer.

Returning to the stern and to my now joyful companion, I left the boatman refuelling Bluebell whilst I gave Scally a quick run ashore and a chance to spend a penny – or more.

I bought another couple of bags of logs plus a bag of coal and after paying for everything I re-started the engine before casting off... another *golden rule*. It is embarrassing to let go the mooring ropes, then find the engine won't start and meanwhile, you've drifted away from the shore and into the middle of the canal!

The boatman kindly let go the forward line, coiling it up and placing it in the well of the bows whilst I re-attached Scally to her chain and let go the aft line.

We needed to turn the boat around but given that Bluebell is 45ft long and the canal is about 30–35ft wide, we had to motor just a little further up the canal to the entrance to the Hilperton Marina.

Here it was possible to swing the boat around, reverse into the marina entrance, then to exit in forward gear – turning east/left back down the canal, the way we had come.

Scally was interested in all that was going on and was not alarmed by all the changes in engine sound, nor by the manoeuvring backwards and forwards.

"Oh, this is such fun, Master! I don't know what you're trying to do, but you don't seem to be able to make up your mind whether you want to go backwards or forwards – and appear to be making a right mess of it!"

She kept swapping sides to make sure she didn't miss anything and was excited by a couple of swans in the marina entrance, barking at them whilst wagging her tail.

This chopping and changing sides again involved my legs getting wrapped up in the chain, but I was beginning to get used to it. I suppose we were training each other in just a few respects!

The journey back to our mooring was uneventful, but we had to overshoot it by about half a mile in order to turn Bluebell around (so that we could moor in the usual way with her stern alongside the landing stage).

We were heading for a "winding hole", the name given to a deliberate widening of the canal to enable boats to turn around.

Turning Bluebell around proved to be a little difficult. A breeze had got up and was blowing down the canal broadside onto Bluebell as I attempted the manoeuvre.

Instead of turning nicely, we ended up nearly across the canal about 20 yards down from where I had started the turn.

However, with firm use of the throttle backwards and forwards I was finally able to bring Bluebell's nose around – to face back up the canal in the direction of our mooring.

Scally had been quiet on our return trip but again took an interest in my attempts to turn the boat around, once more tying me up in her chain!

"Oh dear, he's at it again! I hope he knows what he's doing!"

I gave her a biscuit bone to chew, and she returned to her beanbag in the engine room.

Bringing Bluebell back onto her mooring single-handed was always quite a challenging exercise.

Our landing stage was only about 6ft long, projecting 4ft out from the bank into the canal, with a mooring post further along to which I attached the bowline. Bringing a 45ft boat alongside was fraught with difficulty, let alone then mooring her securely afterwards.

Sometimes my neighbours, seeing me arriving, would kindly come out and help by taking ropes, but I could never always be sure they would be on board.

I had tried it several different ways and sometimes my tactics depended on whether it was breezy and from which direction the breeze was coming.

On this afternoon I was fortunate in that the breeze was coming at me head-on so that Bluebell should be easier to control.

Having put a mooring pin and the mallet handy and checked that the end of the centre rope ran back to my steering position, I throttled back so that we were approaching our mooring very slowly – but with just enough speed to be able to steer the boat.

My plan was simply to motor quietly up to our landing stage, such that Bluebell was kept parallel to the bank, to a point where I could easily step off the stern and onto the landing stage.

I would quickly secure the stern rope to the projecting post of the landing stage, then run up the bank with a spare mooring pin, mallet and the end of the centre rope in hand. The idea was to pull Bluebell close in, using the centre rope (attached halfway along the roof of the boat) and to secure it to the long, permanent mooring pin projecting up from the bank (halfway along our mooring).

If Bluebell was not in just the right position, I would have to knock in another temporary mooring pin to attach the centre rope to, whilst I scuttled back through the boat to attach the bows to the forward mooring post.

Meanwhile, there was a risk of the head-on breeze pushing the bows out into the canal!

All I could do was to try… and to pray for help if I needed it.

I ensured Scally was out of the way on her beanbag, with the aft doors semi-closed on her. Timing would be of the essence and tripping over her chain just as I was stepping ashore could have been disastrous.

It all went surprisingly well, the only problem being that the breeze was indeed trying to push the bows out. Having secured the stern to the landing stage, I had visions of Bluebell swinging right out across the canal blocking it completely – as I raced up the bank, mallet, spare mooring pin and the end of the centre rope in hand.

As it was, it was a close-run thing as to whether I was sufficiently strong and heavy to haul the boat in against the force of the breeze and to get the end of the centre rope secured to the mooring pin.

As a tug of war, my 17 stone was puny compared to Bluebell's 9.5 tons, albeit not dead-weight but floating on water. Thus, we were not exactly evenly matched – and I feared that Bluebell's greater weight would defeat me in the end.

My fellow boaters always take a great interest in seeing how the lone helmsman copes in these situations. So, I was hugely thankful when I was joined by one of my neighbours who had seen my predicament and had come rushing to my aid.

Between us, we managed to tame my almost-runaway-home (complete with my dog attached) and to secure the end of the centre rope to the mooring pin. Thereafter I got Bluebell properly secured fore and aft, turned off the engine and was able to draw breath and take a moment to relax.

We had left the mooring at about 11 a.m. and it was now approaching 2 p.m.

Scally was standing on her bean bag, smiling at me and wagging her tail.

"Well done, Master, that was great! For a moment there I thought I was going for a trip all on my own!"

I took her for a run down our line of moorings to give her the chance to stretch her legs and do her business, then returned to the boat for a late snack lunch.

This was always the part of the weekend I dreaded – Sunday afternoons, heralding the end of our precious time away aboard Bluebell... for another five days.

In an hour or so it would be time to start tidying up the boat, emptying the fridge and packing up in readiness for our return to the flat – and back to another world of surveys, reports and reality.

I suppose I could have moved onto Bluebell permanently and I often toyed with the idea – particularly at this time of the weekend.

After all, she was comfortable, well planned, had plenty of storage space and was warm in winter.

People often used to commiserate with me about how cold the boat must be in winter. However, Bluebell was well insulated and the woodburning stove kept her warm and toastie. I remember one occasion when the accommodation got so hot, I had to go to bed with both the front and back doors open – whilst it was below freezing outside. And that was without using the central heating system!

However, living aboard whilst I was still working was not really practical.

The main issues would have been the 45-minute drive morning and evening between the boat and my office, particularly during the short winter days and given the associated weather... and the lack of any facilities with the mooring.

The provision of a shared wheelbarrow just didn't cut it!

There was no way of replenishing my water supply without a trip up to the boatyard, no mains electrical supply and nowhere to get my laundry done.

I always came back to the same conclusion.

Much as I loved being aboard Bluebell, I had the best of both worlds – a warm and comfortable flat to live in during the week (with laundry facilities and every mod con) and my boat to escape to at the weekends.

I was very lucky compared to many and I should appreciate my good fortune and stop whingeing!

Nonetheless, it was with a heavy heart that I got everything together and took it out onto the landing stage, ready to transfer to the car.

I had let the wood-burner die down but closed off the draught so that the fire would go out naturally and then carried out the remainder of my departure checks – turning off the gas in the bow locker, the water supply under the sink and the fuel supply under the stern.

Scally, bless her, had been fast asleep on her beanbag – conveniently out of my way – while I went through this weekly routine.

However, she was happy enough to have her coat put on, but not so keen to be tied up on the landing stage (in the dark, by now) – whilst I locked the front doors, then turned off the electricity supply from the batteries in the engine room, finally padlocking the back doors and ensuring the boat was secure.

"Come on, Master, what are you playing at? I'm standing here waiting for you, it's dark and it's cold!"

Fortunately, our return load to the car was far less than that when we arrived. There were no logs or bags of coal to worry about, the drinking water canisters were empty, and I had left Scally's food and her beanbag on board.

We trudged along by torchlight, I loaded up with large supermarket bags and Scally on her extendable lead, stopping every now and then to investigate a scent – usually followed by a penny. I reflected that I would always need to keep her on her lead when walking past the boats to stop her spending her pennies on the mooring pins.

But maybe next week I would let her off the lead when walking in the fields near the flat – if perhaps there was another dog for her to play with. We had been so inseparable since I collected her from Birmingham, I really felt there was a bond between us – and the time was coming when I could safely allow her to have a bit more freedom.

The drive home was uneventful, and I passed the time by reviewing Scally's first weekend aboard Bluebell.

I was *so* pleased. Admittedly, put Scally in front of a nice warm fire or under the duvet and she was completely relaxed wherever she was.

But that aside, she had soon got used to getting on and off the boat, we had spent valuable time together on Saturday both on board and during our walk out and back alongside the canal, and she had coped better than I could have hoped with our short cruise today, to and from the boatyard.

It seemed I had picked a *very* special dog, remarkably adaptable and affectionate – and I told her so as we drove along!

***

That first weekend was fairly typical of our weekends together.

Sometimes we just remained on the mooring – whilst I caught up on reports or pottered around the boat doing maintenance jobs. Those were wonderfully relaxed days, getting up late and simply enjoying each other's company – and nearly always going for a long afternoon walk together.

On one of these walks, Scally's constant quest for food got the better of her. By now she was off the lead and free to roam.

She spotted an empty packet caught in a large patch of reeds about 6ft out from the towpath and thinking perhaps it must contain the remains of a pie or something else delicious, she stepped off the towpath to investigate. She got an awful shock when she realised the reeds were not ordinary grass, suddenly finding herself submerged in cold canal water.

"HELP, Daddy! I'm all cold and wet and I can't get out. What's happened? HEEELP!"

I waded in to fetch her out and two very cold and wet souls returned to the boat to dry off and warm up in front of the wood-burner.

"Ooooh, that's better! Thank you for saving me! I was so shocked and frightened."

As the winter days lengthened into longer spring and summer evenings, we took Bluebell out more often, cruising to Bradford on Avon and sometimes through the lock there and onwards up to Dundas Basin at Limpley Stoke.

If we were simply going to Bradford, I would try to find a mooring just before reaching the lock. On this side, there was sufficient space in front of Bradford wharf to turn the boat around for our return journey (so saving ourselves the trouble of having to go through the lock).

It was also possible to take on water this side and there was an excellent little tearoom close to the lock – so that we could watch the boats lining up to go through it, whilst I enjoyed a cup of coffee and shared a cake with Scally.

She was always interested in the passers-by with their variety of dogs, or in looking down into the lock at the boats below from Dundas, passing through it. Bradford is quite a deep lock, so although Scally was always on her lead, I was wary of letting her get too close to the edge. Once the lock gates were closed the water – released by the underwater "paddles" – then lifted the boats higher and higher until they were finally level with us.

Now accessible as far as Scally was concerned, she was always keen to jump aboard the boats to make friends, wagging her tail furiously.

Beyond the lock, the towpath widens out and it was enjoyable just to stroll along looking at the variety of boats usually moored nose to tail, admiring them and chatting with the owners.

There is also a huge, ancient, stone and stone-shingle-roofed empty tithe barn – now restored – beside the towpath about a quarter of a mile out of Bradford, reputed to be one of the largest in the country. It is breathtaking to stand inside it, taking in the enormous space and looking up at the colossal roof timbers high above – whilst imagining its bygone agricultural use and the people and animals of those days who relied upon it.

Sometimes there were no moorings available short of the lock and we would have to take Bluebell through it – in search of a mooring on the other side.

Locks are dangerous places for humans and dogs alike and so – much to her disgust – I would always shut Scally below when negotiating a lock.

There are strong currents when the water is either flowing into the lock or even more dangerously, out of it – beneath the raised paddles – and if a dog fell into the water, it would be sucked down so that it would be well-nigh impossible to save it from drowning.

The other issues are controlling the boat when in the lock – and particularly ensuring that the boat does not get caught up on the sill. These factors apply mostly when the lock is being *emptied* of water, such that the boat drops as the water level drops.

If the boat has been inadvertently tied up to a bollard after entering a lock full of water and the boat drops with the level of the outgoing water, the ropes quickly tighten to a point where they cannot be undone and theoretically, the boat will become suspended – although the lines will probably break under the strain. The boat then drops and there is likely to be significant damage.

(It was for this reason, also to clear anything wrapped around the propeller, that I kept a large carving knife handy in the engine room to cut the ropes in such an emergency).

If the boat is too far back in a lock that is being emptied of water, there is a risk that the rudder and the propeller will be caught on a concrete step or "sill" across the width of the lock. This is invisibly under the water when you enter the lock but is only about 3ft below the surface.

As the lock empties, the back of the boat can become wedged on the sill whilst the front of the boat continues to drop with the level of the water. The boat is then suspended at an angle of some 45 degrees and the front portion is submerged beneath the surface of the water by virtue of its weight.

The water starts to rush in through, or around, the front doors and through holes in the hull normally above the water line accommodating waste pipes etc. The pressure of the water will break the windows and thus the interior becomes swamped.

This is the most common reason for the sinking of narrowboats – and is dreadful to witness.

So, taking Bluebell single-handed through Bradford lock (as the water level dropped) heading towards Dundas Basin was always a bit of a worry.

Often there was a volunteer there from British Waterways (later to become The Canal & River Trust) to help. He or she would close the gates after I had brought Bluebell into the lock, making sure the paddles were lowered/closed at my entry end. The volunteer would then raise/open perhaps only one paddle (to control the outward flow of water) at my departure end.

I would stay on the boat, centre line around a bollard, letting it out as the boat dropped but keeping it fairly taught to stop the boat drifting backwards onto the sill. If I was going through the lock with another boat with a crew, they would often do the paddles.

Sometimes an interested member of the public would be willing to hold the centre line until I had opened the outlet paddle and I would then rush back to relieve them of it, knowing the potential pitfalls and what to do.

If I was completely on my own, I would tie the centre line loosely around a bollard, then race back to retrieve it before the boat dropped too far or drifted backwards onto the sill.

In fact, negotiating the lock always seemed to go without incident for which I was heartily thankful – but it did not stop me from anticipating all sorts of horrifying mishaps beforehand.

Scally was always thrilled to be released as soon as the lock gates opened and we could go on our way.

The only downside with mooring at Bradford is the almost non-existent TV reception – but on the other hand, Bradford has a *great* Fish & Chip shop, there is lots going on and some lovely walks for Scally – including a country park about half a mile out of the town.

Also, it did not take too long to get back to our mooring on Sunday afternoons.

Sometimes we would pass through Bradford on Avon, on our way up to the Dundas Basin.

This is a journey through particularly beautiful countryside, with architecture, woodland and wildlife to enjoy.

About a mile and a half out of Bradford is the Cross Keys Inn, at one end of the Avoncliff aqueduct. This spectacular stone structure is approached around a blind bend and is too narrow to take two boats abreast. So, there was always much sounding of the horn as one approached and often I had to reverse Bluebell to let an oncoming boat off the aqueduct. I soon discovered not to go astern too far as the canal bed on the outer edge of the bend was deceptively shallow and we would then run aground.

Scally was always a fascinated observer, by now wearing a proper lifejacket to which her safety chain was attached and constantly swapping sides to make sure she did not miss anything interesting. I had become a little more adept at avoiding tripping over her chain and it was great to have such an appreciative companion.

I talked to her often, pointing out a duck or a heron, or a dog on another passing boat – telling her *no way* was it as beautiful as her! She wagged her tail and her ears flicked backwards and forwards as I spoke to her.

"Oh Daddy, I don't understand – but you have completely changed my life and made me SO happy. I'm having such fun. Thank you!"

The canal is a fascinating place. There is always nature in abundance whether it be moorhens, ducks with their ducklings, swans with their cygnets, or herons – and occasionally we would hear a woodpecker or see the bright turquoise blue flash of a kingfisher. Water rats and voles live in the banks of the canal and just now and then we caught a fleeting glimpse of them.

There are woods bordering much of the canal between Bradford on Avon and the Dundas Basin. In fact, the canal and its towpath pass through a green "tunnel" of woodland just beyond the Avoncliff aqueduct.

This is stunningly beautiful when the sun shines down through the green canopy of the trees and its dappled shafts of light are reflected as blinding flashes dancing off the surface of the water.

The boats we passed always provided interest, whether they were well-used and loaded character liveaboards, or weekend narrowboats out for a cruise. Sometimes they were on the move, sometimes moored. The liveaboards often had young children and dogs on board, usually playing on the towpath or nearby in the adjacent woods – if their boats were moored up.

Dundas Basin is approached by way of a second, spectacular, aqueduct and I would try to find a mooring just before crossing the aqueduct in case there were no moorings free in the basin itself.

That said, the best moorings are in the basin, particularly on the right-hand side where there is a broad expanse of grass, and the main towpath is opposite on the other side. More space, more privacy!

There was also lots to see.

Dundas Basin is akin to London's Hyde Park Corner when it comes to traffic – in this case, boat traffic comprising craft of all designs, sizes and colour schemes, often nose to tail – travelling down to Bradford on Avon or up to Bath.

However, if the basin is full – and it often is in the summer, with boats moored against the wharf doing a "pump out" and/or taking on water – then one has to execute a right-hand turn out of the basin, passing under a footbridge and now heading for Bath. There are then moorings along the right-hand side of the canal, but one needs to moor fairly close to the basin, in order to be able to reverse back and to turn the boat around.

I always enjoyed my weekends at Dundas.

I had purchased a cabin cruiser in the good times of 2007 (long before buying Bluebell) and she had been moored in the Somerset Coal Canal, accessed from the Dundas Basin.

The Coal Canal was part of the country's canal system, branching off at Dundas and originally extending all the way to Radstock to enable the 19th century barges to collect coal and stone. Thereafter they would return to the Kennet and Avon Canal via the Dundas Basin and thence they headed for Bath or London.

There is an old crane on the wharf in Dundas Basin and nearby stands a former toll house, each bearing testament to bygone days.

The Coal Canal fell into disuse towards the end of the 19th century but the first part of the canal, just off the basin, was acquired during the 1980s by an enterprising and far-sighted gentleman who managed to purchase both sides of the Coal Canal.

Then, with the help of a business partner, they restored it and transformed the Coal Canal into a linear marina with moorings down both sides and a narrow stretch of water down the middle – for boats to pass in or out.

Thus the Coal Canal is now a cul-de-sac about a third of a mile long, extending from Dundas to Brassknocker Basin where boats can turn around, also giving access to the original tunnel under the main road to Bath and which to this day serves as an undercover dry dock and maintenance workshop – the far end being blocked up.

Brassknocker Basin is overlooked by a contemporary semi-circular building constructed as part of the Coal Canal's restoration. This houses The Angelfish Café, also offices for a bike and boat hire business.

When you are thinking of *buying* a boat for yourself, say just for weekend use or for holidays on the water, it is essential to first identify a mooring for it.

I was lucky. My cabin cruiser already came with a mooring in the Coal Canal – a marina which had a very long waiting list for moorings.

During weekends in the spring, summer and autumn, long before I got Scally, my then wife and I would take the cabin cruiser out for an overnight jaunt and so we got to know the Coal Canal and its moorers and staff extremely well.

So, back to the present.

I loved visiting Dundas Basin with Scally, because I had friends nearby in the Coal Canal. It was a good walk for her down the length of the towpath bordering this canal and I enjoyed revisiting the variety of boats moored in the Coal Canal and meeting up with old mates either on board or over a coffee and cake – or maybe enjoying a more substantial lunch – at The Angelfish.

Scally was always welcomed onto the boats, but I had to keep a sharp eye on her – otherwise, she would disappear into my host's bed, under his duvet.

I longed for a mooring for Bluebell in the Coal Canal and had let it be known both to the owner of the canal and to the owner of the boat and bike hire business – who also controlled a few moorings. In fact, I told everyone I could.

I also loved the area around Dundas. It is a stunningly beautiful valley with the River Avon running through it alongside the branch railway line, both bridged by the spectacularly high stone Dundas aqueduct above. This is a masterpiece of 19th century engineering and architectural achievement.

Sometimes the steam train puffs its way through the valley heading down to Weymouth and always draws an audience given the engine's cheerful toot and the smoke coming from its funnel. People appreciate the past, also the tranquillity of the area and the unspoilt woodland and meadow views across the valley.

The Coal Canal is situated roughly midway between Bradford on Avon and Bath. This stretch of the Kennet & Avon Canal linking the two centres passes through arguably the most beautiful countryside of the *whole* 87-mile length of the K&A.

Sometimes I walked Scally up in the woods above the Dundas Basin. She was a young dog then, full of energy and loved exploring the woodland, often disappearing for minutes at a time. I was worried about losing her to start with, but I soon realised she was never far away and always reappeared when I called her, tongue lolling out and with a huge grin on her face – she did smile!

Deer were my principal concern as they could travel miles and Scally's instinct was always to give chase.

They were lovely walks with glimpses, down through a green canopy of trees, of the canal below and of passing boats.

During one uncomfortably hot summer's afternoon, I took Scally for a swim off the pontoon bordering the River Avon – in front of the boathouse serving Monkton Combe School nearby.

I jumped into the water, but Scally was *not* keen, standing right on the edge and whining piteously. She wanted to please me but just could not bring herself to jump in too.

"Oh Daddy, you MUST be joking! You know I can't swim. Don't ask me to do this! I'm frightened".

In the end I grabbed her and notwithstanding her resistance, I pulled her in with me.

"Oh NO! You're not going to do this, are you? OH HELP, you are! I don't like it, I don't like it at all! Please don't make me swim – I'll just sink!"

She struggled to start with but then relaxed in my arms when she became confident that I would not let go of her. I felt rather like a parent teaching a young child to swim.

We had a lovely time together, but whippets are not designed for swimming. Admittedly she was a whippet-cross, but her legs were too thin and her paws too small to be able to push against the water and to swim effectively.

Occasionally we took Bluebell all the way to Bath, a lovely trip passing through Sydney Gardens on the edge of Bath and through a brick-lined tunnel, thereafter under a bridge, supporting a beautiful Georgian house, spanning the canal.

There is a small square hole in the underside of this bridge, down which was lowered paperwork – ordering coal and stone – to the 19th century barges passing just beneath.

These boats were literally horse-powered – or if passing through tunnels without a towpath for the horse, they were powered by the legs of the crew. The crewmen or women and sometimes boys and girls, lay on their backs on the roofs of the boats, "walking" upside-down along the underside surfaces of the tunnels. This was known as "walking the boats through".

If we were going to Bath, I usually took a day's holiday on the Monday, as it was about a four-to-five-hour trip – including passing through the lock at Bradford – to get back onto our mooring at Hilperton. So that gave Scally and I a clear day without cruising on the Sunday, to explore.

By now we had an established routine on the boat.

As the weather became warmer and I used the stove less and less, Scally would crawl under the duvet when I went to bed, and we would snuggle down together.

Mostly it worked well. By virtue of her fine coat, Scally was an exceptionally clean dog and we were sharing a wider than a single bed.

However, she liked to lie stretched out with her back against me and occasionally – paws against the side of the boat – she would stretch her legs as well, in blissful appreciation.

This would propel me across the bed and would result in me suddenly and without warning finding myself clinging to the edge and about to fall into the adjacent passageway!

Upon waking there would be a short early morning walk for Scally to do her business, me usually in dressing gown and fleece-lined builders' safety boots. Then she had her breakfast whilst I washed, got dressed and generally tidied up, before eating mine.

She had got used to my pre-departure routine if we were cruising, lying quietly on her beanbag in the engine room as I went about my chores – instead of her initial anxious barking and whining whilst I was out of her sight.

If we were staying on the mooring and I was doing outside maintenance on Bluebell, I would put Scally on her beanbag up on the bank above the landing stage, tied to a mooring pin. Here she would be safely away from the water and would be able to see me.

She usually settled down quite happily, watching me or snoozing, until somebody walked past. Then she would give them a huge welcome – wagging her tail, rubbing herself against their legs and "talking" to them.

It went down very well with most people who could not get over how friendly Scally was and who made a great fuss of her. Several said how human she was, perhaps the result of us living together and I liked to think because of her feeling of complete security.

Unless the weather turned cold and wet, or I was involved in a long job like repainting Bluebell's roof, we would go out for perhaps an hour and a half's walk in the afternoon – whether we had remained on our permanent mooring or had found a mooring whilst cruising and had stopped for the day.

Scally particularly enjoyed our towpath walks whilst we were away from our permanent mooring.

The liveaboard boats moored alongside the towpath often had young children and dogs on board. These were usually outside playing on the towpath or nearby in the adjacent woods.

Scally was always more relaxed with people than she was with other dogs. In fairness, the dogs were almost always friendly. They had to be, living aboard a boat and spending so much time exposed to the general public on the towpath. Scally was not aggressive, just a lot more hesitant with other dogs – than she was with their owners.

However, once Scally had made friends with their dogs she was always up for a game, particularly if they were lurchers (as they often are) and were willing to run. I was always concerned she would seriously injure a paw on a mooring pin as the dogs chased one another flat out down the towpath, but thankfully she never did.

So, our canal walks were never dull!

Then it would be back to Bluebell, "dinnies" for Scally and a whisky for me, before the evening unfolded.

A New Mooring

Finally, one day mid-week whilst I was in the middle of surveying a roof space, I got a call from Adam – who ran the boat and bike hire business in the Coal Canal.

Did I want one of his moorings in Brassknocker Basin?

He explained he had two moorings free opposite the Angelfish, one of which he had kindly earmarked for me.

I could not say yes fast enough and the following weekend I said goodbye to my friends on the Hilperton moorings and to my landlord farmer – and headed for Dundas.

Some would say it was not a great mooring, lacking privacy right opposite The Angelfish and being so close to the A36 road to Bath, above Brassknocker Basin.

However, I did not mind. I was just so thrilled to be home in the Coal Canal at last.

Actually, it was quite fun seeing the people queuing for the day-boat hire, sometimes hen parties all glamorously dressed up to celebrate for the day, or stag parties usually kitted out as pirates. It was also highly entertaining watching them return, often rather the worse for wear, due to alcohol intake!

The privacy issue did not worry me. I have never been particularly shy, working on the basis that if people do not like what they see, they can always look the other way. Also, they could not really see into my narrowboat as they were on the other side of the canal.

Scally spent many happy hours in the bows watching all the comings and goings – and *loved* our new home.

She would stand there wagging her tail – and whining in frustration as some girl or other talked to her and made a fuss of her from the other side of the canal. Sometimes it all got too much for her and she would jump off the bows, scamper over the nearby bridge and join her group of delighted admirers on the other side – her wagging tail disappearing into a throng of legs!

As for traffic noise, given that the A36 was high above us, most of the noise seemed to go upwards not downwards – and anyway, there is not much lorry traffic at weekends and it is normally quiet in the evenings and at night.

Meanwhile, I had mains electrical and water supplies that I could connect to close by, and Adam let me use his pump-out and sold me gas cylinders. On top of all that there were meals available at the Angelfish Café, opposite. I was like a pig in a mud-bath!

Bringing Bluebell back from a cruise was always an interesting challenge.

Having navigated my way down the narrow Coal Canal without hitting any of the boats, I had to swing Bluebell left-handed as we entered the small Brassknocker Basin, being careful not to clip the back of my neighbour's boat which was moored close to the entrance of the basin, with my stern.

The trick was to steer Bluebell's bows into a "V"-shaped recess cut into the stonework on the Angelfish side, without colliding with it too hard – a fine judgement as I could not see the bows from my steering position.

Then it was necessary to go astern, reversing Bluebell diagonally across the basin, without hitting any of Adam's fibreglass hire boats and theoretically straight into my mooring space almost opposite The Angelfish.

I nearly always attracted an interested audience of tea-and-cake customers sitting at the tables beside the canal, having become quite adept at the manoeuvre – considering Bluebell had a mind of her own when going backwards, as so many narrowboats do.

"Well done, Daddy! Look at everyone watching us… or maybe they're looking at me!"

Sometimes, if I had a lot of reports to check, we would have a lazy weekend, staying on the mooring, perhaps doing a bit of maintenance, meeting a mate at The Angelfish, or hiring a bike from Adam.

Bike riding was great.

The towpaths are always level alongside the canal, and I could go four times as far for a quarter of the effort when exercising Scally. In fact, it was such fun and bike hire was so expensive, that I eventually bought my own bike – a foldaway design that I could store on the boat when not aboard.

I discovered there were two issues with Scally when biking.

She was so excited that she tended to try to grab a peddle in her teeth as I was trying to set off and then she would chase me along the towpath.

"Come on, Daddy! I'm right behind you and I'm faster than you! Pedal, pedal!!"

I did not mind too much, but the game got a bit out of hand when she took to chasing other bikes as well! This was *not* popular with other bikers and had to be stopped.

The effects of talking severely to her and scolding her only lasted until the next temptation and then she was off again in a cloud of dust after her next unsuspecting and startled victim.

"Sorry, Daddy. I know this is wrong, but I just can't help myself! It's such fun!!"

In the end, I had to keep her on her expanding lead as I pedalled along, only letting her off when there were no bikes in sight.

She soon got the idea that when there were bikes around, she would be put on her lead and would lose her freedom. Gradually, over many weekends, she started to lose interest in the chasing game, but it took firmness as well as patience to get her to finally realise that such behaviour made Daddy cross with her and was not acceptable.

The other problem was cats.

Many of the liveaboard boats had a cat and often it would be snoozing outside the boat in the warm sunshine. More often than not Scally never noticed them if they were lying on the roof of their boat.

However, many cats chose to lie in the grass beside the towpath and Scally could spot them from several hundred yards away. If I was not paying attention Scally would be off like an Exocet missile and – having been rudely awakened – the cat would have to take rapid evasive action at the very last minute.

Some owners put notices outside their boats facing both up and down the towpath to forewarn dog owners that there was a cat about, and such notices were helpful, giving me time to put Scally on the lead. Otherwise, I would simply have to apologise profusely – although in fairness most owners were philosophical about it, saying that chasing cats is what most dogs do.

Another Change of Mooring

It was nearly a year after getting back into the Coal Canal that rumours started to circulate that Adam wanted to sell the business – which was then taken over by Bath Narrowboats.

Very sensibly they wanted to increase their maintenance and repair business, given the facility of the dry dock and the workshop in the tunnel.

My mooring was very close by and although I was kindly reassured I could stay on it for as long as I liked, such greater intensity of tunnel use meant many more boats moored around me, waiting to be attended to. It had really become like living right in the middle of a busy boatyard – which it now was!

I mentioned to Tim the owner of the canal, also to Ron our long-standing engineer and the moorer's representative, that I was getting too boxed in by boats and would be really grateful if another mooring could be found for me.

I understand that Ron kindly mentioned my problem to Tim during one of their regular morning meetings over coffee at the Angelfish – saying that I was now "a member of the family" and asking what could be done about it?

Thankfully, this coincided with another boat leaving the Coal Canal and Tim gave me its place.

It was a lovely mooring. I considered it to be one of the best in the whole of the Coal Canal.

Admittedly it was alongside the towpath which was used by the general public visiting the Angelfish as well as our moorers, but it had a fantastic view down the Avon valley and was only about 150 yards from our car park and the facilities of The Angelfish.

I could easily connect to the mains electrical supply, there was a water tap nearby and all the other facilities that I had grown used to were likewise close at hand.

My only concerns were how I was going to stop Scally wandering off – and preventing her from being stolen.

I need not have worried. When it was sunny, she would hop off the bows onto the towpath and sunbathe on the grass close by.

In all the time we had the mooring she never strayed more than 50 yards in either direction, nearly always getting up, wagging her tail and leaning on the legs of any passer-by making a fuss of her.

I kept a close eye on her from the boat, but inevitably I would get engrossed in something – then suddenly come back to reality, thinking "Where's Scally?" in a bit of a panic.

But she was always there, bless her.

Friends from other boats often dropped by for a cup of tea or something stronger and Scally would join us in the bows – excited and pleased to welcome them.

Oh wow! How kind of all my friends to come and see me!

Part Four

Meeting Sandy

I met Sandy on an internet dating website in 2013.

In fact, you could say I met *both* of the ladies in my life on the internet – Scally first, then Sandy.

Sandy and I had each suffered the painful and humiliating indignity of being deserted by our spouses several years before and were hesitant about getting involved too soon.

That said, once we had met, I think we both knew quite quickly there was a good chance that we were going to be together. Scally had shown her usual exuberant welcome, Sandy had responded to her with almost equal enthusiasm, and I was wagging my tail too – metaphorically.

Sandy visited me one Saturday on Bluebell and we went out for a little cruise – down to Bradford on Avon and back. The weather was kind, the countryside looked beautiful and both Bluebell and Scally behaved faultlessly.

We stopped for lunch at The Cross Keys at Avoncliff and ate at a table at the bottom of the steep pub garden, beside the river with the weir nearby and swans close at hand in the water, hoping for scraps.

It was a heavenly day and we each enjoyed one another's company enormously.

Sandy professed herself to be impressed with Bluebell's accommodation and steered the boat without difficulty, having had a narrowboat holiday with a number of girlfriends, when she was younger.

The day ended far too soon – for me anyway – and as Sandy drove away, I hoped that she had enjoyed herself as much as I had. I had not much to offer her in material terms so that the day out on Bluebell was my gift to her, something unusual and I hoped perhaps a bit special.

She called me that evening to let me know she had got home safely and to thank me for a wonderful day – also saying that she would love to do it again sometime if I was up for it. I told her that I was!

Scally had clearly taken to her and although Sandy's family had always had golden retrievers, Sandy seemed to connect to Scally.

I thought about Sandy quite a lot over the next few days, needing to ask myself some serious questions.

I had always assumed that Scally and I would live on Bluebell when I retired, now in eighteen months' time – but would Sandy want to, as well?

If she did not want to live on a narrowboat, then would I be willing to give up my dreams?

And suppose I was willing to do so, how could we possibly afford a place ashore? My pension would not run to paying a mortgage, nor to renting anywhere – and from what I could gather Sandy was living in a rented farm cottage, partly funded by her daughter and son-in-law who were living with her – and had little capital behind her.

I eventually concluded that perhaps my emotions were running ahead of common sense. We needed to give each other far more time before making such lifetime decisions.

All I could do was to invite Sandy to spend several weekends aboard Bluebell and then she could judge whether living aboard would be an option.

Still, looking ahead, I doubted whether she would be prepared to share Bluebell's 4ft bed with a dog as well as a husband!

As the following weeks became months, the initial chemistry between us seemed to grow stronger. We enjoyed one another's company and our times together became more precious, times that we each looked forward to.

Scally and I used to visit Sandy and her family in their cottage on the Somerset Levels midweek and then we would spend our weekends together, mostly on the boat or else at the cottage.

Sandy's family, including Teddy their retriever, made us feel very welcome – part of the family – and they were easy, relaxed and very happy times.

I had to be careful to keep Scally's exuberance under control.

Pip, Charlotte's and Pete's daughter, was two years old. She had been born very prematurely weighing just 1lb 9oz, thereafter spending the first three months of her life in hospital. She was tiny and physically far more vulnerable than most little children of that age.

Scally, who adored everyone but particularly children – being about the same height as little Pip – would have rushed into the cottage and knocked her flat, had I not kept her on her lead until she had calmed down. Scally did not mean her any harm – she was just wildly excited to see her.

She would also help herself to any food left lying around. Teddy was a perfect gentleman and would never steal, but stealing food was in Scally's DNA, particularly Pip's food which was often closer to her height.

The other issue was the family's cats, Phoebe and George. Again, chasing cats was instinctive to Scally so that unfortunately there were one or two incidents early on. I tried my best to forestall such situations and gradually both Scally and the cats became more used to one another – or at least the cats soon realised that Scally was around and kept well out of her way.

However, there was one particularly embarrassing occasion when Scally chased Phoebe down behind the sofa. Not only was Phoebe terrified to come out, but it was a leather sofa and Scally's claws damaged it quite badly.

It must seem that Scally was out of control half the time and completely undisciplined – but that was not the case. In fact, she was a gentle and affectionate soul, obedient and eager to please.

She was just young – best described perhaps in human terms as a good-hearted but immature teenager with a wild streak and it was my responsibility to oversee her behaviour, particularly at critical moments when she was likely to be tempted to do something completely unacceptable.

Dear Sandy, who owned the sofa, was remarkably understanding – indeed her gentleness and her kindness were two of her traits that I had come to particularly respect and to love.

Did I say love??? Yes, we were beginning to realise that there was perhaps a life-changing future and real happiness – within our grasp.

Within six months of meeting one another, we had gone to an antique fair nearby and I had ended up buying a beautiful aquamarine ring for Sandy – an engagement ring. However, we then kept it hidden away for another year or so – as we did not want the family thinking we were rushing into marriage prematurely.

In a sense, the timing was finally decided for us… but that came later.

We continued to spend many of our weekends on Bluebell in the Coal Canal and as our first Christmas together approached, Sandy brought me a Christmas tree – and a wreath to hang on the front doors of Bluebell. This she had beautifully made herself and had decorated it entirely with brussels sprouts, a vegetable she knew I loved!

The Christmas tree sounds a little impractical when you are living with a dog in a steel "cigar case" only 6ft 10ins wide – but it was in fact a green plastic sheet the shape and image of a ready decorated Christmas tree, which we stuck to the side ash panelling in Bluebell's front sitting area and decorated with Christmas lights – brilliant!!!

Scally always gave Sandy an enthusiastically waggy warm welcome and I loved to see them cuddled up together on the dinette in front of the stove – for me, a case of "love me, love my dog" and it wasn't difficult. Scally was such an engaging character. They used to stare into each other's eyes as Sandy stroked her and Scally would double blink as if to say I love you. Sandy would double blink back and this would last several minutes. We called it "the blinking game".

The Flooding of the Levels

As I recall, it had rained steadily during the final weeks of 2013, so that when it continued to rain into 2014, not only were the Somerset Levels flooded but Sandy's village of Muchelney was completely marooned, surrounded by water as far as the eye could see.

When the sun shone, just very occasionally, it was a beautiful sight.

However, all four roads in and out of the village were impassable due to the floodwater. There was an almost submerged car on the road between Muchelney and Langport which had not made it through, and it stayed there beneath the water with just its roof exposed – a sorry sight – for nearly eight weeks.

Supplies were brought in by boat and the church became a distribution hub. This continued until the floodwaters finally receded and the roads were reopened, after nearly two months.

Meanwhile firemen from several stations – also others – ferried villagers to and from Langport in a rubber boat to collect their cars parked on the "mainland", so that they could drive to work or go shopping.

This kind service also facilitated our ongoing courtship!

Both Scally and Teddy loved the little boat, crammed in as they were with parents, children, other dogs and the two firemen on duty. It was even more of squash on the way home, with all the shopping bags full and often I would travel with Scally in my arms, as she stood on the edge of the rubber boat.

She always seemed rather superior, experienced as she was with water travel!

One afternoon, the fireman in the bows stood with his arms out behind him, humming the theme music from Titanic! They were consistently cheerful and kind, volunteering to give up their precious free time to ferry us backwards and forwards, a trip which took a good 15–20 minutes each way – and they never stopped from 7:30 a.m. until darkness fell, every day.

Towards the end of this period, when the floods had subsided a little, a former Army "duck" was brought in. This was a tracked vehicle, apparently semi-submersible and very noisy to travel in.

Scally was amazingly trusting and apparently unconcerned, sitting on my lap and leaning against me as she looked out of the windows at the expanse of water and at all the birds it attracted.

"Yay, Daddy, this is good! I can see SO MUCH from up here, so many ducks and geese and swans. Maybe we could bring the boat down here and live closer to Sandy's village?"

Sandy and I were much more concerned, knowing there were 6ft deep water-filled ditches, or "rhynes", on either side of the road, completely concealed from view by all the water and into which we might tip at any moment. We sat there trying to plan our escape if we suddenly tipped over.

On the Move

Soon after the end of the floods Pete and Charlotte started to think about buying their own house, whilst prices were still just about affordable.

Pete was now established as a graphic designer and in a secure job. The cottage was tiny and he and Charlotte would obviously welcome the privacy and greater space afforded by a family home of their own. Given that Pete was now earning enough for them to fund a mortgage, they talked to Sandy about their plans and then started looking for somewhere else to live.

It was not long before they found a property, and this prompted Sandy and I to think rather more seriously about our own future.

There was no doubt in our minds – we wanted to be together.

The immediate question was, where are we going to live?

Continuing to rent the cottage was not an option. We could not afford it and anyway it held too many unhappy memories for Sandy.

I had come to realise that living permanently on Bluebell would not work for Sandy and the more time Scally and I spent with her, the less I minded.

Her stepfather had sadly died shortly before Sandy and I had met and providentially had left her a legacy in his will, enough to buy a flat – or even a wide-beam canal boat!

In fact, we viewed a lovely one near Devizes. It was luxuriously spacious and fitted out and we could have lived on it very comfortably.

However, Sandy suffers from fibromyalgia, a very painful condition affecting her muscles that comes on when she is tired and/or cold. So, although it is easy to keep warm on a boat, living on the water is several degrees colder than living on land. This would have triggered more fibro attacks.

Besides, the canal was a little over an hours' drive from Sandy's family and being devoted to them, Sandy felt she wanted to be nearer – within say half an hour away, at the most.

So, we started to look.

We submitted offers on two possible properties, one after another, but each proved to have legal or other practical complications and we had to withdraw.

I then kept noticing a converted first floor flat in a village within our search area, regularly advertised in the paper. The Edwardian house it was in looked solid and full of character and so we went to look at it.

The flat was lovely, far exceeding our expectations.

It had a wide and spacious living room at the front-facing west for the afternoon and evening sun and with a lovely outlook, behind this a large double bedroom facing east for the morning sun, whilst still heading backwards there was a modern bathroom, then a refitted kitchen right at the back. This overlooked a rear yard and had a back door opening onto a wrought-iron balcony and staircase leading down into a good-sized, shared rear garden.

There was a wonderful view of Ham Hill and of the monument on the top, from the balcony.

I think I also liked the flat because it reminded me of living on a narrow boat!

The garden arrangement suited us fine. It was shared between four flats so that we would not be solely responsible for cutting the grass and looking after the garden generally – leaving us time to visit Bluebell in the Coal Canal.

As it turned out only Sandy and I and one other occupant, used the garden on a regular basis – another bonus.

We ended up buying the flat, having first discovered the roof needed re-slating – paid for by way of a price reduction – and carried out soon after we moved in.

After living on Bluebell or at Sandy's cottage, Scally loved the extra space and particularly the garden.

"Oh Daddy, this is perfect! Lying on a comfy sunbed in the sun, in our own garden!"

The previous owners of our flat had a cat so that there was quite a large cat-flap inset to our back kitchen door. At that time the weather was cold, and Scally was sleeping in a knitted "pullover" in her basket in the living room, with the run of the flat during the night.

One morning, I opened the back door from the kitchen and there was Scally's pullover lying in a little heap on the balcony. I was intrigued, until it dawned on me that she must have been quietly pushing her way out of the cat-flap during the night, to enjoy a taste of freedom in the garden!

Sandy and I had been wondering why Scally was regularly suffering an upset tummy, whilst one of our neighbours had likewise been wondering where all the cat food, she had been putting out every night for a hedgehog, had been disappearing to.

Two of our neighbours had cats. We had to check that the coast was clear before we let Scally out of the back door, and she would then stand on the balcony with a bird's eye view of the garden. If she saw any movement, she threw herself down the steps and hurtled up the garden barking as she went – which was embarrassing whenever she found a cat to chase.

However, one day the tables were turned. Our kindly downstairs neighbour had just taken on an elderly cat from a friend who had sadly died, but who used to live in our block.

This tiny black cat was *not* going to put up with any of Scally's behaviour. The cat bravely stood her ground, hissed and spat at a startled Scally and then proceeded to chase Scally around the garden.

This was exactly what Scally needed and from that day on the cat used to sit at the bottom of our steps into the garden and Scally was too frightened of it to slink past. If she tried to, she would get spat at and scratched.

Part Five

Selling Bluebell/Buying March Hare

It was now clear I would not be living full time on Bluebell anytime soon – or at all, for that matter.

Sandy and I enjoyed our weekends aboard and our trips down the Kennet & Avon Canal. However, Bluebell was costing me £250 per month – in mooring fees to keep her in the Coal Canal, for the Canal & River Trust licence and for general maintenance – including blacking the hull every two years, involving taking her out of the water.

Very shortly I would be retiring, and all this would then have to be paid for out of my rather meagre pension – and would be unaffordable.

Of course, keeping Bluebell would have worked financially if I had been living on her full time – but I wasn't. And now I had to cover the overheads of running an establishment ashore as well. How my life had changed!

That said, I did not regret my change of lifestyle, nor such additional expenses – for one moment.

I now had a lovely wife-to-be, with whom I was sharing a small but comfortable character home. I felt truly happy and very fortunate.

There was an additional reason for considering selling Bluebell.

On many occasions when I went to stay on her, my keenly anticipated visits were spent doing unexpected maintenance. Things go wrong on a narrowboat if she is not being used regularly and you need to live aboard full time to keep on top of everything.

I have said it before – in respect of the woodburning stove – but caring for a narrowboat is also rather like looking after a two-year-old child. The moment your back is turned, there is another problem to deal with.

So, selling my beloved Bluebell was therefore becoming not merely a possibility but more a looming necessity – for financial as well as practical reasons.

It was a tough decision that I did not want to take.

Like Scally, Bluebell had seen me through some difficult times and had brought me a lot of fun, good friendships and happiness. And now I was facing the prospect of losing her.

Three things helped me to make the inevitable decision.

First, I had been extremely lucky to have had the experience of owning such a lovely narrowboat and she had given me some wonderful memories.

Second, I was now anticipating a very different and a *much* happier future than the future I was facing when I had bought Bluebell.

Third, I discovered there was a chance of buying back my old cabin cruiser March Hare – the one that I had owned before I bought Bluebell – and still with a mooring in the Coal Canal, amongst my friends.

I knew all her foibles and how to look after her and she is a fibreglass boat requiring far less maintenance than Bluebell – a steel boat. She is 22ft long instead of 45ft long and thus my expenses would be more than halved.

I had only to put my head into March Hare's cockpit and cabin to recall her old smell and I was pretty well sold on the idea!

I did the deal with the owner Gareth, managed to sell Bluebell successfully to a family who clearly loved her and moved my things across onto March Hare.

She is a Freeman, a vintage boat over 50 years old, solidly built, pretty and much of the accommodation is lined in mahogany.

We were in a different part of the Coal Canal, which I promptly christened "Paupers Corner", set aside for less expensive, smaller "yoghurt pots" – as our fibreglass boats were disdainfully referred to by the narrow boaters.

From Scally's point of view, this relocation involved accessing March Hare, not by way of a nice wide towpath and hopping easily aboard at much the same level, as she was used to with Bluebell.

Instead, access was along a very narrow metal pontoon between two closely moored boats on either side, then necessitating an agile leap by Scally of 2ft 6ins up onto March Hare's side gunnel and thence into the rear cockpit.

She was OK with hopping on and off the boat, but she did not feel confident on the metal pontoon. The surface was slippery, the boats were too close to one another on either side and the pontoon and space available were too narrow for her to turn around if she changed her mind.

She was *not* impressed!

"Oh Daddy, I don't fancy this! I'm frightened. WHAT have you done, getting this boat and selling our lovely Bluebell? I just can't understand you!"

Early on she tried to reverse backwards and fell into the water. I heard the splash and found her with her back half immersed and her front half above water – her front legs across the pontoon and clinging on for dear life.

Poor girl! I felt *dreadfully* sorry for her.

I got her out very quickly, dried her off and gave her some doggy treats. Next day, after I got home, I went into a popular store selling goods cheaply and bought nine rubber car mats for £1 each.

Once these were laid over the pontoon, Scally got her confidence back and thereafter trotted happily along it, hopping on and off March Hare without too much difficulty.

Taking her out for her last penny was always a bit scary, particularly if it was dark. I had a good strong torch and I had her on the lead in case she should fall in. I dreaded this – the idea of her losing her footing and getting stuck in the water *under* the pontoon. So I was always relieved when we returned, safe and sound and she hopped agilely into the rear cockpit and then made her way down into the cabin.

Also, there was no wood-burning stove on March Hare.

We did have an electric heater and Scally would spend the evenings – and sometimes winter afternoons – in her fur-lined coat on sheepskin beanbags, covered by my dressing gown often with my anorak on top. She slept like that on the starboard side bunk, whilst I occupied the port-side bunk – in the front of the boat.

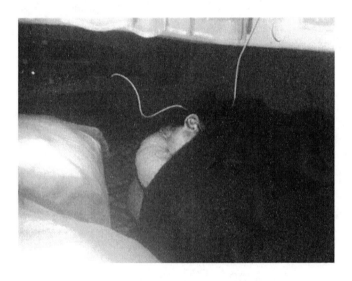

"Mmm, this is SO comfy and warm! Maybe this boat isn't so bad after all!"

It was cosy and intimate in that I was close to her and if she lost her "over-blankets" during the night I could just reach across and put them back on top of her. I marvelled at her skill in turning over or turning around whilst keeping her coverings in place and it was rare that I would hear a little whimper to tell me she needed help.

If it got too cold, I could also reach over and switch on the heater which stood between us.

She was not yet an old dog, but she was starting to suffer from arthritic joints. I had her on tablets to ease the problem, but when it was time to go outside for her last penny before bedtime, she was so stiff I had to rub her shoulders and her haunches to get the blood flowing before lifting her down off her beanbag. Then she was ready to hop up into the rear cockpit and off the side of the boat.

She needed more of my attention on March Hare than she had on Bluebell – given the access issues and the absence of a stove to keep her warm.

Whilst I had always spent my days anticipating her needs and thinking of her welfare, now I needed to take even greater care of her in many respects.

Physically we were living at closer quarters to one another on March Hare and I think we became psychologically closer too. I talked to her a lot and she would listen to me with her ears cocked, wag her tail and occasionally "talk" back.

"Daddy, I don't know what you're trying to tell me, but I love you talking to me. You make me feel very loved and cared for – and protected. Thank you!"

She also seemed to understand our more restricted space.

There was not enough room in the cabin for both of us when I was getting up and so as soon as I got out of my berth Scally immediately moved across and crawled under my duvet!

"Oh YESSS!!! This is what I've been waiting for – ALL night!"

I was not so naïve as to think she was being helpful – she wanted the warmth of the duvet!

Nonetheless, she was happy to stay there for ages without chivvying me for her breakfast – and when she was hungry, she slipped through to the rear cockpit and lay patiently on the cross seat until I was ready to feed her or to take her out.

"C'mon Daddy, where's my breakfast? I'm starving!!!"

During the summer months when we were outside much more, I would get engrossed in some maintenance job on March Hare, but Scally never wandered off. As before when Bluebell was moored alongside the towpath, Scally never strayed more than 50 yards from the boat. I was always grateful for this.

The only occasion I lost her was in the middle of the night.

She woke me with her whining, standing in the aft cockpit with her nose pressed against the side flap, which was clipped closed. She wagged her tail when I appeared whining all the more. Sleepily I let her out, as I had done on such previous occasions, thinking she was probably desperate for a poo. She had always returned, within a few minutes.

However, 10 minutes went by. I called her, but she did not appear.

I was starting to get worried. I realised I had let her out without her collar on and the main road to Bath, although quiet at this time of night, was not far away. I had visions of her getting run over or stolen.

I pulled on some clothes and my boots and with my torch and her lead went in search of her.

There was no sign of her nearby around the boats, nor at the head of the track leading up to the main road – and at that point, the gates were shut anyway. I walked down to the Dundas Basin calling for her – then back along the track leading to the car park, below The Angelfish.

I thought she could be there, going through the café's refuse or eating the remains of some cake or pie left on the ground by a customer… but no luck.

I walked back along our towpath and over the bridge to Pauper's Corner, calling all the while – but again, there was no sign of her.

By now I was getting *very* worried, trying to keep my rising panic under control.

I decided to again walk up the track, this time right up to the main road – as there was a garage with a convenience shop only 100 yards along the road. Scally might have found something interesting to eat there.

I was just halfway up the track when to my immense relief the light from my torch picked out Scally trotting down it towards me.

She was licking her lips and shamefacedly wagging her tail.

"Oh Daddy, PLEASE don't be cross with me. I could smell something LOVELY, even from inside the boat and I had

142

to go and investigate. I heard you calling, but I couldn't drag myself away. I'm sorry… it did taste nice, though!"

She knew perfectly well she had been naughty. She got a heartfelt ticking off, slinking away down the track and back along our pontoon – where I found her waiting to be let on to March Hare.

Next morning, I walked her up the track and through the gates, intending to turn right and to head down to Dundas Basin for a walk along the canal.

However, Scally was intent on turning *left* and just around the corner, in the gateway of the next house, was a torn-open rubbish sack with part of the contents strewn across the drive, including the remains of a chicken carcass.

This was almost certainly Scally's handiwork, so I felt compelled to put everything back in the sack and to ram it into a corner so that the torn portion was difficult for a fox (or a dog) to get at. Luckily, the refuse lorry was due to collect the rubbish that day.

Now all I had to do was to await the digestive drama of a chicken bone stuck in Scally's gut – but miraculously she seemed to get away with it.

***

Sandy and I always enjoy giving our friends a day out on March Hare – a trip down the Kennet & Avon canal to include a picnic aboard, or a pit stop at The Cross Guns at Avoncliff.

Shortly after Scally's midnight disappearing trick, Sandy brought dear Val, one of our neighbours, up to the canal for a day out to celebrate her upcoming birthday.

She's a lovely lady in her late 70s', forever cheerful and a wonderful example of growing old gracefully – with a great sense of humour and a naughty twinkle in her eye. We are very fond of her.

For any boat to leave the Coal Canal and so enter the main Kennet & Avon Canal at Dundas Basin, a member of the crew needs to remove the padlock from the metal lift bridge separating the two canals. They then lift this small, hinged bridge by way of chains, to allow the departing boat to motor through the gap beneath the bridge and into the basin.

Sandy kindly did the honours and at the last moment, Scally hopped ashore to be with her.

There were a lot of boats about so that I was restricted both in time and space to get Sandy and Scally back aboard. I retrieved Sandy, but Scally was distracted by another dog, a similar whippet-cross and would not come when called.

So I set off, taking March Hare across the aqueduct, thinking Scally would catch up – which she did, racing past us and waiting at a point the other side to be picked up.

This was a hopeless place to get in close to take her aboard and so we motored on past her looking for a better pick-up location.

I think this must have triggered a memory in her brain of being abandoned as a puppy – and I shall *never* forget her horrified and panic-stricken howl of anguish and despair as we continued along the canal, seemingly ignoring her, without stopping to pick her up.

As it happened the "ice cream boat" was moored a little further on. Scally knew it well, having had her own very small vanilla cornet from there from time to time. I was able to moor alongside the boat and Scally, any idea of another ice cream completely forgotten, hopped across his stern and back onto March Hare, tail wagging and "talking" and "talking" with outpouring relief.

I was dreadfully upset at having heard that pathetic, helpless wail of anguish – the thought that she believed that I, of all people, was dumping her.

However, I could not help thinking she had given me almost as bad a fright a couple of nights earlier!

Part Six

Our Other Holidays Afloat

For the past four years, my brother Mark, his son/my nephew Jamie and I have hired a boat, just for a few days, in order to explore Britain's waterways further afield.

Mark always brought Higgins, his border terrier whom he often referred to as "the border terrorist" when introducing him to other dog owners.

I always brought Scally.

The first year, in 2017, we explored part of the Monmouth and Brecon Canal in a narrowboat.

The weather was bright and sunny for the most part and the Welsh countryside was beautiful.

However, the canal was narrow and needed dredging, so that if we met another boat coming the other way one of us would inevitably run aground.

Partly as a result, we kept getting rubbish around the propeller shaft – often discarded heavy-duty plastic agricultural feed sacks. To clear these, we needed to ensure the ignition was turned off, then to remove the top of the weed hatch in the engine bay – thus giving us direct access to the prop shaft and to the propeller itself, immediately below.

Then, it was a matter of reaching down into the water to cut away or to unravel the obstruction.

The feed sacks were our regular culprits, but sometimes it was sacks made of jute, lengths of rope, old washing up cloths and items of clothing. Our most amusing find was an enormous black bra wrapped around the prop shaft, itself wrapped in some old jute sacking. We had some fun speculating how they came to be together!

So, it was always a matter of conjecture between us as to what we would find next when the engine suddenly stopped.

Higgins and Scally were always fascinated spectators, joining a row of upended bottoms to peer down through the weed hatch, to see what was going on.

The two dogs got on with one another very well – given that they only ever met usually once a year.

Higgins slept with Mark, in the bow cabin, where he had his basket.

I slept in the saloon with Scally – who either slept on her beanbag or under the duvet with me.

This arrangement suited both Mark and I – as we each had independent access to the outside of the boat if we had to let the dogs out during the night.

By day, the dogs often cuddled up together sharing the same bean bag on deck or would stand on the edge of the stern to look at the passing countryside and to see where we were going.

However, we had to be careful to keep them well separated at feeding time.

Higgins was not slow in coming forward to investigate what Scally had in her food bowl – even when she was eating. This was just too much for Scally to tolerate and what sounded like a full-blown dog fight would then ensue. That said, blood was only drawn on one occasion.

Scally was just as bad given half a chance – but she was sly in her approach. She would wait until Higgins was up on deck before finishing anything that was left in his bowl.

So, Mark and I quickly realised that the dogs needed to be strictly separated at feeding time and their bowls were removed as soon as they had finished eating.

Obvious really – but we were each used to looking after only one dog, each of whom behaved perfectly when by themselves.

The only other thing our "Mon and Brec" holiday was memorable for – apart from some great times together – was that poor Mark fell into the canal.

It was a classic case of trying to get ashore to moor up and the bows of the boat moving away from the bank as Mark was getting off. With a foot on each, the usual "splits" ensued followed by a shout of dismay and a loud splash.

Mark took it very well, seeing the funny side and was licked almost dry by a very concerned Higgins.

***

In 2018 we decided to explore part of the Llangollen Canal in North Wales.

There was no music festival at the time of our visit, something we understood the area to be well known for, but the Pontcysyllte Aqueduct more than made up for it. This is an 18 arched stone structure supporting the canal water in a 5ft deep metal trough on top. The aqueduct spans the River Dee and at 1007ft long it is the longest aqueduct in Great Britain and at 126ft high, the highest in the world – completed in 1805.

We kept the dogs below when crossing it.

On one side is a tarmac towpath bordered by 5ft high close-fitting vertical metal safety railings.

However, on the southern side, there is *nothing at all* – merely a 5-inch-high upright metal lip between the top of the canal trough holding the water and the 126ft sheer drop into the valley below.

The aqueduct is only wide enough to carry one-way traffic, but even so there are only a few inches between the hull of the boat and the lip on one side and the towpath on the other.

We crossed the aqueduct twice, given our outward and homeward journeys and it was a spectacularly memorable experience on both occasions.

We also went through a long one-way tunnel, understood to be 1381ft in length, completed in 1802.

Again, Higgins and Scally were banned to the cabin below.

We could not risk one or both of them falling overboard in the pitch-black tunnel – lit only by the spotlight in our bows, or by our torches.

The tunnel has a very slight bend in it, so that it seemed an age before we could finally see a pinprick of light in the distance, far ahead of us – giving a literal meaning to "seeing light at the end of the tunnel".

We emerged into almost blinding sunshine bathing the beautiful Welsh countryside in bright white light.

Some of the way, the canal is inset to the contours of the hills, with views over the valley below. Here, the canal is narrow though provided with "passing bays", allowing oncoming boats to pass one another.

This was more spectacular countryside than that of the gentler rolling hills and pastures bordering the Monmouth and Brecon Canal, which we had explored the year before.

Both Higgins and Scally were quite relaxed both on and off the boat. Higgins, with shorter legs, found jumping on and off the boat more challenging – often helped by Mark – than the longer-legged Scally who negotiated the gap between the boat and the bank without hesitation.

Of course, most of the time they were "landlubbers" – Higgins living in a large apartment in Mark's case, although with daily walks alongside the Thames nearby. Scally, although living at home, was more of a water dog – having spent so many of her weekends first on Bluebell, then latterly weekends as well as longer visits on March Hare.

***

Hitherto we had only hired narrowboats, but in 2019 we hired a wide-beam for our four-day trip together – a luxury apartment on the water.

And this time we were on the much wider Thames with masses of space around us.

We picked up "Georgia" in Caversham, a beautiful 62ft long x 12ft wide vessel painted Oxford blue and equipped with bow thrusters for manoeuvrability.

There was a huge cabin in the bows giving outside access which Mark and Higgins had, a large bathroom divided this from Jamie's cabin with an en-suite loo and then the rear half of the boat opened up into a lounge, a dining area and the galley – though the latter was the size of a spacious domestic kitchen ashore.

I slept on the sofa bed in the lounge, so that Scally and I had direct access onto the enormous stern in case she needed to go out during the night.

Before we set off, Scally and Higgins had their usual set-to without damaging one another – more a case of establishing the pecking order – and thereafter behaved as firm friends, again sharing a bed out on the stern as we cruised along.

I'm not too sure I enjoy sharing my bed with this "so-called" friend!

We had decided to explore the Thames going downstream, two days out and two days back giving us four nights aboard.

We passed through Sonning and Shiplake where Jamie had been at school and had spent much of his time rowing up and down the Thames.

Next came Wargrave and then the beautiful old town of Henley on Thames. Here we saw a stretch of the river being prepared for the Henley Regatta, due to take place several weeks ahead. Part of the course had been roped off and marquees and stands were being erected alongside.

After passing by peaceful water meadows, we admired the riverside towns of Marlow and Maidenhead, soon afterwards turning around just short of Bray for our return trip.

We had found some great overnight moorings, with lovely pubs/restaurants nearby, that we visited – taking Scally and Higgins along too. If the dogs were not welcome, we simply went elsewhere.

One afternoon we identified a little pub to visit that evening – which involved mooring Georgia alongside a very rickety-looking landing stage sticking out into the Thames at right angles.

We tried to moor Georgia to this, slowly motoring her up to it – but each time the current took us back downstream. On the 3rd attempt, we took Georgia upstream of the landing stage and let the current float us down onto it – risking demolishing the timber structure altogether.

This strategy proved much more successful and to our surprise, the landing stage stood firm as we gently bumped alongside it.

Just as we were tying up and congratulating ourselves on a successful manoeuvre, a barge came into view travelling upstream at quite a rate of knots. At the last moment, it turned in to moor on the downstream side of the landing stage – as we had unsuccessfully attempted.

Reducing speed only a little, the boat headed for the landing stage at an angle of about 40 degrees, its bows running aground just short of the bank.

Suitably "anchored", the helmsman then put his helm hard over, revving his engine and swinging his stern in to lie snugly alongside the structure.

It was an impressive demonstration of boat handling in a tricky situation, and we heartily congratulated them over dinner later that evening, in the little pub just up the track from our landing stage.

We usually stopped travelling at about 4:30 p.m., to give us time to take the dogs for a good walk along the towpath.

They loved this time of day, freed at last from the confines of the boat and able to enjoy the chance of chasing each other up and down the towpath, exploring lots of interesting smells and trying to board other people's boats – at least Scally was always keen to do so. It came from having a boat of our own and to her, it was the most natural thing in the world to hop aboard, tail wagging enthusiastically – much to the surprise of the owners.

We would then return to Georgia, feed the dogs and enjoy a drink or two together whilst planning the next day's itinerary, before heading out to supper.

***

Due to the Coronavirus our four-day trip in 2020, originally planned for mid-April, had to be delayed until the last couple of days of September and the first two days of October.

We had decided to hire Georgia again, this time exploring the Thames upstream.

This would take us through Pangbourne where I spent many happy afternoons sailing GPs or Fireflies – sailing dinghies – at the Bradfield College Sailing Club, one of my escapes from school.

This stretch of the Thames was also used by the racing rowers of The Pangbourne Nautical College. Strictly speaking, power should give way to sail but they never did – resulting in some potentially expensive near-misses and a lot of very satisfactory shouting.

As we motored past, I was able to identify the old oak tree on the bank that we used to climb, then from there we would drop from an overhanging branch into the Thames below, to cool off on hot summer days.

Further upstream we came to Goring and Streatley. Mark and his wife Julie had bought a beautiful old house on the Thames in Goring and it had been their family home as their three children had grown up. From its garden, there is a wooden footbridge that takes you onto quite a large island in the Thames, also part of the property.

Jamie knew the current owners who kindly invited us to visit on our return trip and it was fascinating to see what changes had been made since the "Weedon era".

From Goring and Streatley we headed north, passing the little village of Moulsford. This was of particular interest to me because here there is a small boatyard where they maintain Freeman cabin cruisers – and I had visited them the year before to get March Hare's water pump repaired and overhauled.

It is a wonderful set-up. Even though many of the Freeman boats are now 30 – 50 years old, you can still email the boatyard for spare parts and telephone them for helpful maintenance advice – always enthusiastically given.

Pushing on, we passed the lovely old town of Wallingford. Here our grandparents had rented a charming little Georgian house close to the waters' edge. Our mother had left from there to marry our father in 1948.

We got as far as Shillingford before having to turn around for the return leg.

It was another great trip – the three of us were good for one another.

Mark was our honorary skipper both by virtue of his age and because he kindly organised the hiring of the boats.

I was more often than not the helmsman given my practical experience with boats.

Jamie was the cabin boy, given his youth and greater physical abilities and without his help and kindness to his fellow old duffers, the trips would not have been as fun and easy as they were.

It was Jamie who leapt off the boat taking mooring lines and securing us – and it was Jamie who dealt with the locks we had to pass through. All were electrified (unlike those on the Kennet & Avon Canal), but not all were manned at that time of year and Jamie became our "Lock-expert".

The dogs, too, remained good friends.

That said, they had quite a meaningful dog fight on the last morning just as we were handing back the boat.

Due to Covid restrictions and regulations, we had to have everything packed and ready to take off the boat, the moment we arrived back in Caversham.

I think the dogs were unsettled at seeing all our bags lined up and ready to go. After all, it is easy for us humans to know what's about to happen – we've organised it!

But not so for a dog. It thinks that maybe it is going to be left behind (and when I had all my bags packed at home, ready to take to March Hare for a few days, Scally always stuck to my side like a little limpet).

On this occasion, the dog fight necessitated a visit to the vet when I got home – but no serious harm was done.

Part Seven
Our Life at Home

We live in a wonderful place for doggy walks, just under Ham Hill.

Our routine was that first thing every morning I drove Scally up to the top of the hill. She would do her business and then we would explore the variety of paths – Scally stopping and sniffing at the latest wildlife smells from overnight. She also loved eating all the "chocolate raisins" that the bunnies had left during their dawn breakfast!

There were a lot of other dog walkers out at that time of day and Scally became well known and popular.

She would gallop up to people, her tail wagging furiously. She always slowed down before she reached them then, lifting her front legs, she would "prance" the last few yards to meet them. She would rub herself against their legs and I could swear she was always smiling. If they bent or squatted down, she would "kiss" them with enthusiasm, much to their surprise.

Few dogs openly show such affection, but Scally always loved people.

Those who knew her, seeing her in the distance, would throw their arms wide calling "Scalleeeee" and she would instantly respond, tearing up to them with her little "prance" of delight as she joined them.

Often Sandy would join us and then we would adjourn to The Prince of Wales pub on the top of the hill after our walk, for a cool drink in the summer, or for hot chocolate or a coffee in the winter.

Being located at the start and finish of so many walks the pub is hugely popular with walkers – and welcomes dogs. In fact, sometimes there are as many dogs in the bar as people.

The staff consider the dogs as customers too, selling biscuit bones as well as drinks, also providing a hose down outside and numerous freshly filled water bowls.

During the first Covid lockdown from late March until early June 2020, I had been recuperating from a prostate operation. However, by early May I was well on the mend – but cars were not allowed to be used to get to good walking areas and so were banned from the hill, also from many other such areas locally… and of course, the pub was shut.

So, missing our walks on the hill, I decided to try walking with Scally up from the village below, starting on the road, then branching off onto a path around the flank of the hill, but sloping ever-upward. This was quite a steep climb, a slope of some 30 degrees in places.

Aged 70 and not very fit after my operation, I was not really expecting to reach the top. So, as we set off together, my intention was to take it slowly. I would keep putting one foot in front of the other and would simply see how far I could get.

Scally ran ahead investigating new scents as I plodded along in her wake. She would never run too far ahead of me on any walk, often stopping and looking back to make sure I was there – and this walk was no exception.

I finally stopped for a breather and to admire the view of the village below and of the countryside beyond. It occurred to me that this was a similar view to that from the monument right on the top of the hill. I turned and looked upwards and there it was – just over my right shoulder.

We had made it to the top!

We repeated that walk several times and it became a favourite of ours.

The top of the hill was originally a Saxon hill fort so that there is a "rampart" walk all around the outer edge with fantastic views, another of our favourites.

Later, the hill became a stone quarry and to this day the landscape is constantly changing as a small quarrying operation continues.

In the year 2000, the quarry owners erected a circle of large upright stones in the centre part of the top of the hill to celebrate the centenary. Here they light a bonfire on November 5th – but to my heartfelt approval fireworks are banned!

Scally and I sometimes attended outdoor Remembrance services at the monument on or close to November 11th. Locals both drive and walk up from the village and the congregation at the monument is swelled by others visiting from Yeovil and elsewhere. It is an informal yet moving service with both a piper and a bugler to honour the dead, as wreaths are laid around the monument steps.

Scally seemed to know this was a special occasion lying patiently at my feet, as other dogs whined and pulled at their leads – wanting some action.

This memorial was a favourite destination for our walks, and we were often joined by Sandy.

Other times, Scally enjoyed exploring the woods around the base of Ham hill – shady walks during the hot summer months and a different set of scents for her.

Occasionally, I would slip and fall during our walks on the hill, where sometimes the path was particularly steep and slippery with mud.

It was never dramatic. I never hurt myself physically. It was merely my pride that took a tumble!

Scally's reaction was immediate. She would *rush* back to me to make sure I was alright, giving me masses of kisses as I sat there in the mud – and if I laughed, she would think it a game, jumping all over me and preventing me from getting to my feet.

Our afternoon walks were usually around the village with Scally mostly on her extendable lead – although there were places where I could let her off it to enjoy greater freedom.

These were walks through the apple or soft fruit orchards, around some of the arable fields or otherwise down to the millennium wood with its lake nearby – often accompanied by Sandy.

Scally seemed to enjoy these walks almost as much as her time on the hill and developed friendships with a whole new set of dog walkers. She got on pretty well with other dogs – but it was the people with whom she really connected.

***

Sometimes Sandy, Scally and I would visit Lyme Regis, together with the rest of Sandy's family, for a day out including a picnic on the beach. It was only some 40 minutes' drive from where we all lived, and it held some very happy memories for Sandy and I.

One sunny day I had popped the question to Sandy on the end of the cobb which part encircles the harbour in Lyme Regis – and to celebrate our engagement we went out to lunch afterwards in a nice seafood restaurant. We then sat on the promenade with our legs dangling over the edge, watching the holidaymakers on the beach and wanting to tell everyone of our happiness.

We were eating ice creams and an enormous seagull flew down from behind us and before we realised what was happening, he was flying away with Sandy's cornet in his beak!

So, the seaside town was a special place for us and for Sandy's family.

Pete and Charlotte's young girls Pip and now Ettie adored paddling, rock-pooling or making sandcastles and Teddy, the family's golden retriever who now lived with them, was a natural water dog.

Esme (Sandy's younger daughter) and Jamie (Esme's partner) nearly always came too, later accompanied by Oscar. Oscar was a handsome red retriever puppy adopted by Esme and Jamie and he was to become another "seadog".

Loving the sea, Teddy spent much of his time running in and out of the water fetching a red rubber ball, sticks, or lengths of seaweed that we threw into the sea for him to retrieve.

Scally, however, was not a water dog, but even she would go down to the waters' edge and paddle in the small gentle waves that lapped onto the beach. She would occasionally chase Teddy if he was teasing her with a particularly inviting looking stick, or otherwise simply enjoyed running in and out of the water with the family.

Pip and Ettie would build their sandcastles with moats of seawater, always decorated with stones and seashells from the beach. Tiring of this eventually, they would then paddle or swim in the sea with their Dad Pete – followed by a picnic lunch.

The girls adored the dogs. When they got wet, the girls would wrap them up in coats and towels in case they were cold, on the winter days that we visited Lyme.

Even before the picnic was unpacked Scally was right there in the centre of things – coats and towels suddenly discarded – in case there was the remotest chance of being given a bit of sandwich or part of a sausage. In fairness, she was really quite well behaved – anxiously watching us, but never moving unless she was offered a morsel.

Come on! I'm starving, after all that running in and out of the sea!

She loved those days out with all the family – her own special collection of people.

Scally Misdemeanours

There were times when we visited Steve and Irene who lived near Petersfield – friends of Sandy's and now my friends too – and Scally was always invited.

Sandy was particularly close to Irene as they had gone to school together and were inseparable in those days.

We were staying overnight as usual – in fact for a long weekend.

Their son Ollie was still living at home but was out the afternoon we arrived – and going on to a party that evening – so that we did not see him until he surfaced for a late breakfast, next morning.

He came down to the kitchen looking a little the worse for wear – and rather shocked.

He had woken to find a strange dog that he had never met before, cuddled up against him under his duvet!

***

Scally made a name for herself on another occasion.

Sandy and I regularly attended St Cleers Chapel on a Sunday morning. It was Sandy's place of worship when I met her, and I was inspired by my very first attendance – and thereafter.

Several months later we left Scally locked in the car as usual, windows part down, in the shade under the trees, whilst we attended the church service. She was perfectly safe – it was not a hot day.

We had recently had the car serviced and MOT'd – and I had not had time to re-erect Scally's cage in the back.

So, she was free to roam within the car – as it were.

When we got back into the car to go home, I was rather surprised to find the short inner end of my seatbelt loose in my hand – no longer attached to the floor.

Sandy then discovered her seatbelt wet and partially chewed through – and upon further investigation, we found the two outer seatbelts in the back were also both now badly frayed and damp.

Scally was looking hangdog and very guilty – and I then realised her bed on the back seat now had a hole in it.

"I'm really sorry, Daddy. I couldn't help myself. I was SO frightened. I was trying to get out and to run away".

We never quite knew why Scally had wrought such damage.

There had been no thunder or lightning to frighten her whilst we were in the chapel worshipping – at least we had heard and seen nothing to indicate a storm – and the ground outside was still perfectly dry. Anyway, it was not that sort of weather.

We eventually concluded that Scally must have been upset by the noise of a train or trains going past the chapel car park – just over the wall – and she had been frightened, thinking the noise was thunder.

She was evidently upset at what she had done, and I was not going to punish her if she had been terrified by something which maybe we should have anticipated.

Actually – I was secretly quite impressed by Scally's intelligence.

Clearly, she wanted to run away from the noise but could not escape from the car. She had seen Sandy and I undo our seat belts and open the doors and perhaps Scally had reasoned that if she gnawed through the seat belts then the car doors would open, enabling her escape. After all, she never touched the rear centre belt!

I was not quite so laid back when it came to replacing the seatbelts.

In spite of spending long hours on the popular websites, I was only able to track down one second-hand seatbelt for my make of car – but I needed four.

In the end, the total cost was just over £1000 and the entire car had only cost me £2000 to buy!

Thereafter, Scally got left at home on Sunday mornings lying happily on our duvet, often beneath it once we had safely departed – and she never did any further damage.

On those occasions, upon our return she would meet us at the top of our stairs, wagging her tail in welcome, often pawing at us to say hello.

She would then run ahead of us into the kitchen and with a loud and surprisingly commanding "woof" would stand with her nose pressed against the door of the cupboard where her biscuits and treats were kept… as if to say.

"I've been good and looked after the house. Please can I have a reward?"

She had other foibles too.

She spent much of her time asleep on her back in her bed, on the sofa, or on our bed. She seemed to find it a wonderfully relaxing position.

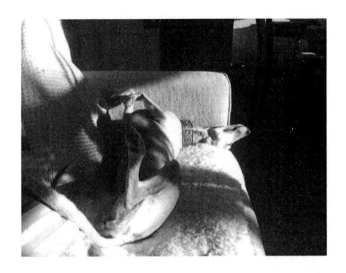

Another foible would be to stand up on her hind legs on our bed or on the sofa in our sitting room, with her front legs around my neck (or Sandy's), her chin on my shoulder. I would scratch her back from behind her neck all the way down to her tail and back again – and she would groan in ecstasy, as I told her that I loved her.

"Oh Daddy, THAT'S total bliss! Please don't stop. I could stand here all day while you do that. Just a bit lower and to the side – Oooh, that's wonderful!"

I would say, "Daddy *loves* you! Yes, Daddy *loves* his Scallywag! You're a *very special* girl!" and I would be rewarded with a big wet kiss!

I often said this when we were out on our walks together and she would prance up to me in delight and rub herself against my legs.

Every morning when I got up, it was my job to make Sandy's tea and my coffee. Whilst waiting for the kettle to boil in the kitchen, I would go into our sitting room where Scally would either be wide awake or snoozing in her basket (later, we bought Scally a single duvet of her own – and she *loved* it!). I would draw back the curtains and then bend down to fondle Scally's ears and to tell her she could now come and join us in bed.

Sometimes she would get up and trot through to our bedroom and on those occasions, I would find my side of the bed occupied – by a large lump under the duvet – when I returned with our early morning revivers.

A certain amount of shifting of deadweight dog was then required – accompanied by groans of protest at being disturbed, as I tried to get back into bed.

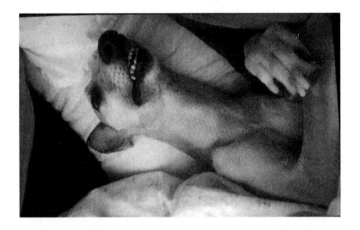

Later, having become too hot, Scally would do her usual thing of clambering out of the head of the duvet, then turning around to face the foot of the bed. She would flop down with her back legs stretched out towards us, flat on top of the duvet to cool her tummy, presenting us with her bottom. We had to hang onto our end of the duvet, otherwise, this manoeuvre would result in Scally taking most of the duvet with her.

Other times Scally would carry on snoozing in her basket in the sitting room, later suddenly appearing around our bedroom door to join us in bed. She would take a flying leap over the foot of our bed and usually lie down on top of the duvet just out of our reach. She would then whimper and whinge until we had dragged her closer to us so that she could have her tummy tickled.

On these occasions, Sandy and Scally would often play the blinking game. If Sandy stopped tickling her Scally would blink at her, Sandy would blink back and so the game continued until Scally became even more desperate for a tickle and moved closer, within easier reach.

She would also blink at us for attention when we were watching the telly in the sitting room.

Come on, you two! I'm waiting for some attention. I'm much more interesting than that TV you're glued to!

She would lie in her bed on her duvet and stare at us. If we took no notice she would whimper, then start blinking and we would blink back, telling her how much we loved her. That seemed to satisfy her – at least for a while!

Part Eight

The Final Curtain 3rd December 2020

It was about 08:45am as I drove the courtesy car home from the garage. Our car was having its annual service that day.

My phone rang. I ignored it but it rang again, then a third time. I thought I had better find out who it was, trying to get hold of me with such determination.

Sandy's name was on the screen.

"Where are you," she asked.

"About five minutes from home," I replied – knowing full well I was a good 15 minutes away, but I did not want to have to stop at the village shop and to queue up to buy groceries that Sandy may have forgotten to get earlier in the week.

"Scally's breathing is terribly fast. and her heart rate is much too high. I think there's something very wrong with her".

My heart skipped a beat. "OK," I said. "I'll be with you as quickly as I can," putting my foot hard down on the accelerator.

I walked into our bedroom to find Sandy lying on the bed cuddling Scally, who was part under the duvet in her usual position. I could see her ribcage rising and falling much too quickly to be normal and from her expression, she was obviously distressed and frightened.

I was lucky. The vet would see Scally straightaway.

Given the Covid precautions, I had to hand Scally over to a youngish lady vet at the entrance door.

Poor Scally. She has always hated going to the vets, ever since she had her claws clipped when she was much younger and the vet cut through the quick, making her yelp and bleed.

She tried everything to avoid going through the door, but eventually gave in. I was told they would phone me just as soon as they had diagnosed the problem… but it was not until 8 p.m. that evening that they were finally able to tell us what was causing Scally such discomfort and distress.

Initially, after the vet had carried out numerous tests on her which revealed nothing seriously amiss, I had collected her at lunchtime.

She was still breathing fast but not quite so dramatically fast as earlier in the morning. They thought it could be a pancreatic problem and told me we should keep her warm and quiet.

"Bring her back later if you're still worried about her" I was told.

Scally spent the afternoon on our bed with Sandy, part under the duvet, with Sandy's hot pad over her, having her head and her tummy stroked and she slept a little – but there was no improvement by 5:30 p.m.

So, after calling the vet again, I took Scally down to the surgery once more.

This time I was met by a brisk but motherly lady vet who asked me to sign a consent form for an X-ray and once I had handed over Scally I was told to go on home. She would call me.

At 8 p.m., she phoned us. It was serious. The X-ray had revealed that one of Scally's lungs had collapsed. They had drained air from her ribcage and had re-inflated the lung – but within just a few minutes it had collapsed again.

The vet suggested that she should call the specialist vets at Langford (near Bristol) to see if they would carry out an emergency operation. We agreed and she said she would call me back.

This gave Sandy and I the chance to consider what to do – to put Scally through what must be a major operation or to put her to sleep.

We were in shock. Scally had always been a perfectly healthy dog right up to that morning. She had suffered no traumatic accident likely to have caused a serious internal injury – and yet here we were, out of the blue, suddenly having to consider euthanasia.

Back on the line, the vet said that the vets in Langford would take Scally. However, with the lung collapsed our vet told us she could not see where or why it was leaking air into the ribcage and the most likely explanation was that some form of malignant growth or polyp had perforated the lung lining.

Further, without accurately identifying the cause of this crisis, even after the operation the lung could collapse again – particularly if it was a polyp issue.

Lastly, we should understand it would be a brutally traumatic procedure – following a lengthy car journey to get Scally there.

My mobile had been on speaker-phone so that Sandy could hear the conversation. Having asked the vet to hang on for a moment, we agreed that Scally was almost 10 years old, she had had a wonderfully full, active, happy and healthy life, the outcome was dodgy, to say the least and it sounded like a horrible operation. We did not wish to put her through it, and had no choice but to have her put to sleep.

Back on the phone and having heard our decision, our lady vet told me I would need to come down to the surgery. She had to have another Consent form signed and although it was against their Covid protection rules, she would let me in to hold Scally whilst she administered the fatal dose.

She met me at the front door. She had the Consent form ready which I signed. I felt I was signing Scally's death warrant, which I suppose I was – but she told me we were doing the right thing, given the circumstances. She would have done the same. She then led me through the building, opening swing doors into what appeared to be a large operating space, with a smaller room off it.

Scally was lying in a large open cage on the floor, a blanket over her and a sheepskin beneath, on top of some sort of bean bag. She looked warm and comfortable – and a bit sleepy.

However, she recognised me straight away and tried to get up – but then lay back on her sheepskin and her tail wagged weakly.

I knelt in front of her and took her head in my hands. I stroked the top of her head and her wonderfully soft ears, telling her gently to "stay", and that it was "time for bye-byes". I told her she would feel better in a minute. "Just go to sleep now, there's a good girl. I'll stay with you. You're quite safe".

The lady vet asked me to move to one side for a moment, to give her room to attach a line to Scally's foreleg where there was a small brightly coloured bandage and presumably an intravenous connection. Then she stepped back behind me.

All the while, Scally never took her eyes off my face, even for a moment. She looked at me so intently with such joy that I was there with her, and with such a depth of love in her eyes.

She was clearly drowsy and relaxed – but awake and trying to respond to my presence. All she could really do was to blink at me, and I blinked back in reply – the game Sandy and I often played with her, in our case to tell her how much we loved her – and vice versa, Sandy and I imagined.

After a moment some liquid flowed down the line. The amazing thing was that Scally kept her eyes on me throughout, even after she started to relax. I laid her head gently back on the sheepskin.

It was over.

Epilogue

In the hours and days following Scally's death, Sandy and I were in shock.

It had come upon us so suddenly and without warning that we were completely unprepared for it.

Just the day before we had been walking with her on Ham Hill. She had got a little left behind whilst investigating an interesting scent. She had then come rocketing past us flat out – like an Exocet missile – taking the steep slope up the grassed rampart nearby in just three strides.

I had commented then how lovely it was to see Scally run, her zest for life and that she was really in pretty good shape for a dog of her age. She stood above us, waiting for us to catch up – her tongue lolling out, just smiling down on us with her tail wagging.

Now, we felt heartbroken.

Scally became *our* dog when we got together, and Sandy had her own special relationship with her. They spent a lot of time cuddling on the bed together, given Sandy's fibromyalgia and Scally's love of both attention and the duvet!

But it was I who adopted her and brought her up in the years before I had met Sandy, and before I had retired. It was I who mainly walked her morning and evening, mostly fed her and took her to the boat with me, first on Bluebell then on March Hare for our little holidays together and on cruises elsewhere.

So I was *devastated* – there's no other word for it.

Scally came into my life at a time when I had lost almost everything and she had been my loving companion nearly all *her* life – giving me wholehearted affection, joy, and a fresh focus every day.

I simply could not believe that we would not see Scally again.

We missed her most when we returned to the flat, having been out shopping or been to church. No longer was she standing at the top of the stairs, tail wagging and smiling, waiting to welcome us.

No longer did she come into our bedroom each morning for a cuddle with us, on the bed.

In the days that followed Scally's death, I walked all her favourite walks on Ham Hill and around the village, both to "lay her ghost" and in the hope that she might suddenly appear to me – even if it was just for a moment.

If I got up in the night to go to the bathroom, I would go into the living room in the hope of finding Scally snoozing on the sofa, waiting for me. In fact, I still do – and probably always will.

And before going to bed I would check that she was not waiting outside the back door to be let in.

I could not bear the thought that she might have come back to visit, and I had ignored her.

I tried to be brave and to comfort Sandy, but more often than not it was Sandy comforting me.

In short, I had *never* known such grief before, even following the death of family members.

I told myself to get a grip – to stop being so wet.

I had been an army officer in HM forces, for goodness' sake. I had been through the tough Sandhurst training and had led and cared for each of the 30 men of my troop, under my command. I used to say that although the army was not my ultimate career, I was glad of the training and of the experience. It meant I could always cope with anything life threw at me.

Well, I'm ashamed to say I didn't cope very well with the loss of Scally.

Thinking about it, I suppose Scally was like a child to me. She gave me her total loyalty, trust and love in the knowledge that I would care for her.

So, every day it was important to me to ensure that she was safe, secure and happy. It became second nature to me.

Yes, I spoilt her sometimes but so what? Most of the time there was just the two of us and she knew the boundaries.

I talked to her a lot, and she was more responsive than any other dog I had owned or known before.

She was enormously outgoing and affectionate, both with other people but especially with me and Sandy.

She seemed to know when I was busy, and when she needed to either give me some space on the boat or to amuse herself when I was working outside – without wandering off.

When other walkers admired her and asked about her breeding, I would always tell them she was a whippet-cross and what an easy dog she was to live with – obedient, affectionate and fun to be around.

That said, I know that every dog is special.

This little book is written to honour *our* special dog and to preserve her memory. Scally was a loving companion and friend who gave us her all and who, for a number of precious years, so brightly illuminated our lives.

You love them, but you don't realise quite how much until they're gone.

I hope that if you have a dog, you may experience the same affection and joy that Scally gave to Sandy and I.

A Postscript

Just after I had finished writing these final lines, their content unknown to Sandy, she came through from the kitchen where she had been preparing lunch.

She told me through tears of joy that she had just heard a voice in her head.

"Tell him I'm honoured he's writing a book about me".

I showed her what I had just written, and we were both stunned.

Scally's spirit had found a way of sending me that message through Sandy – and bless her, now I *know* she lives on!

Yesterday I found Richard Gale's letter, my vet's reference that I took to Birmingham with me, to satisfy Miss Athill that I would be a suitable person to give Scally a home.

The letter was folded up in the back of my much-used book of road maps, along with several other items of discarded paperwork. I had slipped it into my map book when I left Birmingham for the drive home, eight years ago and had forgotten it was there. Hence why it looks so worn.

Date: 16ᵗʰ January 2012.

Ref: Mr. C. Weedon of 33 Homecanton House, Carrington Way, Wincanton, Somerset
BA9 9JH.

To whom it may concern,

Mr Weedon has been a client of Southill Veterinary Group for over ten years. He is an
experienced dog owner who has always taken exceptional care of his animals. He has
never hesitated to seek Veterinary advice when concerned about his animal's health and
is always diligent in implementing any recommendations.

I can wholeheartedly recommend him to you as an ideal candidate for a new dog and can
assure you of his pet-owning credentials.

If I can be any further assistance please do not hesitate to contact me.

With kind regards,

Mr. R........ Gale MA VetMB CertVC MRCVS

...mere   milborne port   gillingham
...1226   01963 250255   01747 82...
...www.southillvets.com...

185